INDIAN REAL ESTATE DECODED

A HOMEBUYER'S GUIDE AND CAREER LAUNCHPAD

SAURABH BAJETHA

For Those Who Light My Path

To Dadaji,
I hope you are watching me from above, guide me on this journey.

To Dadi, Papa, and Mummy,
Every step I take, every milestone I achieve, is to make you proud. Your blessings and support mean everything.

To bhai and behen,
No matter where life takes us, I'll always be there for you both. That's a promise.

And to my friends,
Who've stood by me through my darkest hours and know me better than I know myself—you know who you are. Thank you for everything.

With love,
Saurabh

Contents

PREFACE

Why This Book Matters

The Indian real estate market is one of the largest and fastest-growing sectors in the world. Whether you're a first-time homebuyer, a real estate investor, or an aspiring entrepreneur, understanding how to navigate this market is crucial for making informed, profitable decisions.

This book, "Indian Real Estate Decoded: A Homebuyer's Guide and Career Launchpad," is designed to be your comprehensive guide to everything you need to know about buying property, investing wisely, and building a successful career in real estate.

Who Is This Book For?

✓ Homebuyers → Learn how to choose the right property, negotiate prices, secure financing, and avoid legal pitfalls.

✓ Real Estate Investors → Discover how to build a profitable property portfolio, maximize rental income, and time the market for high returns.

✓ Real Estate Entrepreneurs → Explore career opportunities, start a real estate business, or leverage PropTech innovations to succeed.

✓ NRIs & Global Investors → Understand how foreign investment works, tax implications, and the best cities to invest in.

Pro Tip: Whether you're buying your first home or your tenth investment property, this book provides expert strategies to help you make the best financial decisions.

The Importance of Real Estate in India

Real estate is not just about homes—it's about economic growth, job creation, and wealth building.

✓ By 2030, the Indian real estate sector will reach $1 trillion, contributing over 13% to India's GDP.

✓ Urbanization is rapidly increasing, with Tier-2 and Tier-3 cities becoming major investment hubs.

✓ Government policies like RERA, REITs, and 100% FDI in real estate have made the sector more transparent and investor-friendly.

This means the best opportunities in real estate are happening right now—and this book will help you take advantage of them.

What You Will Learn in This Book

This book is structured into 20 detailed chapters, covering every critical aspect of the real estate journey:

✓ Buying Your First Home → Step-by-step guidance on choosing the right location, financing options, and legal checks.

✓ Investment Strategies → Rental income, property flipping, commercial real estate, and REITs.

✓ Market Trends & Cycles → How to time the market, buy low, and sell high.

✓ PropTech & AI in Real Estate → Learn how technology is reshaping the industry.

✓ Career & Business Opportunities → How to become a real estate broker, developer, or PropTech entrepreneur.

Pro Tip: This book is a blend of practical insights, case studies, and expert strategies to help you navigate India's complex real estate landscape.

How to Use This Book

✓ Read it cover to cover for a full understanding of real estate in India.

✓ Jump to specific chapters based on your needs (e.g., financing, negotiation, investment).

✓ Apply the strategies—real estate success comes from knowledge and action.

Final Thoughts: Why Now Is the Best Time to Invest in Real Estate

The Indian real estate market is evolving fast. With new policies, infrastructure projects, and PropTech innovations, the opportunities today are better than ever.

✓ Homebuyers can find great deals with RERA protection & competitive home loan rates.

✓ Investors can capitalize on Tier-2 city growth, rental demand, and commercial real estate expansion.

✓ Entrepreneurs can leverage PropTech, digital platforms, and AI-driven real estate solutions.

Pro Tip: The best real estate decisions are made with the right knowledge—and this book will equip you with everything you need to succeed.

Let's begin your real estate journey!

Hey there! If you're reading this, you must be thinking, "Why, out of all the books, did I pick this one? Who is this guy?" Well, let me be very clear—I'm not an expert (not yet, anyway). I'm just a knowledge seeker like you who was desperately looking for a guide to navigate the labyrinth of Indian real estate.

When I couldn't find one, I thought, "How hard could it be to write one?" (Spoiler alert: Pretty hard!) My journey started at Amity University, where I spent years studying civil engineering, convinced that knowing the tensile strength of concrete would somehow make me a real estate wizard. Surprise, surprise—real life had other plans. In 2016, fresh out of college with a degree that made my parents proud and a head full of theoretical knowledge that was about as practical as an umbrella in a hurricane, I landed my first job as a Graduate Engineer Trainee.

That's when reality hit me harder than a poorly mixed batch of concrete. Since then, I've worn many hard hats—from a Site Engineer squinting at blueprints to a Project Engineer at a PSU, and now, an entrepreneur trying not to look completely lost while running my own real estate venture. I've negotiated with contractors who could smell my inexperience from a mile away, solved construction crises while pretending to know exactly what I was doing, and somehow managed to not accidentally demolish anything important (yet). But here's the thing—throughout this comedy of errors that I call my career, I noticed something. Everyone in real estate seems to be either completely clueless or pretending to know everything. The middle ground? As rare as a property dealer who returns calls on time.

I wrote this book because I wished something like this existed when I was starting out—a no-nonsense guide that doesn't assume you were born knowing what FSI means or that you can decipher property documents written in what appears to be ancient Sanskrit. Whether you're a student dreaming of building cities (bless your optimistic soul) or a family looking to invest your life savings without having a nervous breakdown, this book is my attempt to share everything I've learned the hard way.

Consider it your cheat sheet to avoiding the mistakes I made and making interesting new ones of your own. I'm still learning, still making mistakes, and still occasionally googling basic construction terms when no one's looking. But if there's one thing I know for sure, it's that real estate doesn't have to be as complicated as we've made it.

So, let's figure this out together. After all, if I could survive and thrive in this industry with nothing but determination, a degree, and a slightly concerning addiction to coffee, imagine what you could do with an actual guide in hand. Welcome to " Indian Real Estate Decoded: A Homebuyer's Guide and Career Launchpad "—because someone had to write it, and apparently, that someone is me.

— **Saurabh Bajetha** (P.S. If you're wondering whether buying this book was a good investment, well... at least it's cheaper than a square foot in Mumbai or Gurugram!)

I

The Indian Real Estate Landscape

"The land is where our roots are. The rest of the world is just a marketplace."
— Indian Proverb

1.1 The Evolution of Indian Real Estate

A Journey from Tradition to Modernity

Imagine a time when buying a home wasn't a financial decision—it was a family tradition. In the pre-independence era, land was often passed down through generations, and property transactions were based on trust and verbal agreements rather than legal contracts. Fast forward to today, and India's real estate market is a complex ecosystem of urban expansion, government regulations, foreign investments, and digital transformation.

Real estate in India has evolved through three distinct phases:

Phase 1: The Pre-Liberalization Era (1947–1991) – The Age of Scarcity

The post-independence period was marked by:

• Government-Controlled Housing Policies – The introduction of the Urban Land Ceiling Act (1976) restricted private land holdings, limiting property development.

• State-Driven Housing Projects – Development authorities like DDA (Delhi Development Authority) and MHADA (Maharashtra Housing and Area Development Authority) dominated housing supply.

• Minimal Private Sector Involvement – Real estate was not yet seen as a business sector, and infrastructure development lagged behind growing urban populations.

Challenges:

✔ Chronic housing shortages – By 1980, India faced a 19-million-unit housing deficit.

✔ Strict rent control laws – Mumbai's Rent Control Act (1947) froze rental prices, creating artificial housing scarcity.

✔ Limited financing options – Home loans were difficult to obtain, and interest rates were as high as 18%.

Phase 2: The Post-Liberalization Boom (1991–2010) – The Golden Age

The 1991 economic reforms opened India's doors to foreign investment, private developers, and financial institutions, leading to:

• The Rise of Private Developers – DLF, Hiranandani, Unitech, and other real estate giants emerged.

• Growth of IT & Commercial Hubs – Cities like Bengaluru, Gurugram, and Pune transformed into real estate powerhouses.

• Housing Finance Revolution – The emergence of HDFC, ICICI, and SBI home loans made property ownership easier.

Case Study: Gurugram's Rise

In the 1980s, Gurugram was nothing more than farmland. By 2000, thanks to the entry of MNCs, Cyber City and Golf Course Road became India's prime commercial hubs, driving residential real estate prices up by 400% in a decade.

Phase 3: The Modern Regulatory Era (2010–Present) – Transparency & Digital Transformation

Since 2010, India's real estate market has seen a shift towards transparency, compliance, and digital integration, driven by:

• RERA (2016) – The Real Estate (Regulation and Development) Act introduced accountability, reducing builder fraud and project delays.

• REITs & Foreign Investment – India's first Real Estate Investment Trust (REIT) was launched in 2019, attracting global investors.

• PropTech & Digital Transactions – Platforms like NoBroker, MagicBricks, and 99acres have revolutionized real estate buying and renting.

1.2 Urbanization & Infrastructure: The Growth Engines

By 2030, India will have 600 million urban residents, driving a demand for 25 million new homes worth ₹1.5 trillion.

The Urban Shift: A New Era of Growth

• Mumbai, Delhi NCR, and Bengaluru continue to dominate the luxury and commercial real estate markets.

• Emerging Tier-2 cities like Indore, Jaipur, and Coimbatore are witnessing rapid price appreciation due to industrial growth.

Case Study: The Dholera Smart City Project

Dholera, a previously undeveloped region in Gujarat, is now positioned to become India's first planned smart city, expected to attract ₹1 lakh crore in investments and generate 100,000 new jobs.

1.3 Government Policies: Reshaping the Market

RERA (2016): The Game-Changer

• Mandatory project registration to eliminate fraudulent builders.

• 70% of funds must be kept in escrow accounts to prevent mismanagement.

• Standardized definitions of carpet area to prevent misleading advertisements.

✓ Impact: By 2023, 78,000 projects were RERA-registered, and consumer complaints resolution rates reached 65%.

PMAY (2015): Affordable Housing for All

The Pradhan Mantri Awas Yojana (PMAY) aims to provide 1.2 crore affordable homes with:

• Credit-linked subsidies of up to ₹2.67 lakh per homebuyer.

• Tax benefits for first-time buyers.

✓ Impact: PMAY has helped 35% more first-time buyers enter the housing market.

The GST Effect

• Under-construction properties attract 5-12% GST.

• Ready-to-move homes are exempt from GST, making them more attractive to buyers.

✓ Result: A shift in demand from under-construction to ready-to-move properties.

1.4 The Future of Indian Real Estate

Top 5 Real Estate Trends for the Next Decade

1. The Rise of Tier-2 and Tier-3 Cities

• Infrastructure projects like Delhi-Mumbai Expressway and Chennai-Bengaluru Industrial Corridor are shifting demand to smaller cities.

2. Digital-First Real Estate Transactions

• PropTech startups are transforming property searches, legal verifications, and even AI-powered price predictions.

3. Co-Living & Co-Working Spaces

• Flexible working trends are driving demand for managed rental properties and hybrid office spaces.

4. Sustainable & Green Buildings

• Homebuyers are willing to pay 5-10% more for green-certified buildings with solar power and rainwater harvesting.

5. AI & Blockchain in Property Transactions

• Smart contracts will reduce fraud, making property title transfers faster and tamper-proof.

Key Takeaways

✓ Real estate is cyclical – Understanding past trends helps predict future growth.

✓ Government policies like RERA & PMAY are making homebuying safer.

✓ Urbanization will continue driving demand, especially in Tier-2 & Tier-3 cities.

✓ Digital tools and AI are revolutionizing the way properties are bought and sold.

What's Next?

In Chapter 2: Legal Safeguards for Homebuyers, we'll break down property laws, title verification, and fraud prevention strategies to protect your investment.

Did You Know?

Real estate's fascinating history stretches back millennia. The earliest recorded property transaction was documented on a clay tablet in Mesopotamia (modern-day Iraq) around 2900 BC. This ancient deed of sale, detailing the purchase of a field and house, reminds us that real estate has been central to human civilization since its earliest days.

II

Legal Safeguards for Homebuyers

"Knowledge of the law is the first armor against exploitation." — Legal Maxim

2.1 Why Legal Knowledge is Essential in Real Estate

Real estate fraud is more common than most people realize. A 2023 study found that 45% of consumer court cases in India are related to real estate disputes.

Case Study: The Noida Twin Towers Scam

• In 2010, a group of buyers invested in a high-rise project by a reputed developer in Noida.

• The project promised state-of-the-art amenities and RERA compliance.

• By 2016, it was discovered that the building had violated environmental and zoning laws.

• 2022 Verdict: The Supreme Court ordered demolition of the towers, and over   ₹600 crore of buyer money was stuck in litigation.

Lesson: Even reputed builders can engage in malpractice. Buyers must personally verify legal documents before investing.

2.2 Key Legal Documents Every Homebuyer Must Verify

Before signing any agreement, you need to legally verify that the property is free from disputes and meets government regulations.

Checklist: Essential Legal Documents for a Property Purchase

1. Title Deed (Ownership Certificate)

• Confirms the seller's legal ownership.

• Must be verified through the Sub-Registrar's office.

• Red Flag: A property cannot be sold if it has multiple ownership claims.

2. Encumbrance Certificate (EC)

• Confirms the property has no unpaid loans or mortgages.

• Obtainable from the local Registrar's Office.

• Red Flag: If a loan is unpaid, the bank can seize the property—even if you've bought it.

3. Sale Agreement

• Should include: final price, payment schedule, penalty clauses for delays, and refund terms.

• Red Flag: If the builder refuses to include a refund clause, it's a warning sign.

4. RERA Registration Certificate

• Required for all projects larger than 500 sq. meters or with 8+ apartments.

• Search your project's RERA ID on the state RERA website (e.g., MahaRERA, UP RERA).

• Red Flag: Unregistered projects have no consumer protection rights.

5.Approved Building Plan & Land Use Certificate

• Ensures that the project follows zoning laws and has received municipal approvals.

• Obtain from the local Municipal Development Authority.

• Red Flag: Illegal constructions are subject to demolition orders.

6. Occupancy Certificate (OC) & Completion Certificate (CC)

• OC = Confirms the building is fit for occupancy.

• CC = Confirms that construction complies with government approvals.

• Red Flag: If a builder gives possession without an OC, the home may be legally uninhabitable.

Pro Tip: Use Digital Verification Tools

Many Indian states now allow online property record searches. Websites like Dharani (Telangana), Bhulekh (UP), and E-Governance Karnataka provide online land records.

2.3 Common Real Estate Scams & How to Avoid Them

1. Illegal Land Sales (Selling Without Clear Title)

• Fraudsters sell land without valid ownership or by forging title deeds.

• Prevention:

✓ Always check the Encumbrance Certificate and verify ownership at the Sub-Registrar's Office.

2. Delayed Projects & Fund Diversion

• Developers collect money but delay construction, using funds for other projects.

• Prevention:

✓ Invest only in RERA-registered projects.

✓ Visit previous projects by the developer to check past delivery records.

3. Fake Promises & Hidden Costs

• Advertisements promise "free parking, gym, and club membership" but later charge extra for these amenities.

• Prevention:

✓ Demand written confirmation of all inclusions in the sale agreement.

4. The "Assured Returns" Trap

• Some builders offer guaranteed rental returns on properties, but fail to honor the contract.

• Prevention:

✓ Verify if rental guarantees are legally enforceable.

5. Forged NOCs & Illegal Approvals

• Some projects fake municipal approvals to speed up sales.

• Prevention:

✓ Always check Municipal Corporation approval documents in person or online.

2.4 How RERA Protects Homebuyers

The Real Estate (Regulation and Development) Act (2016) provides buyers with legal protection against builder fraud.

Key RERA Protections

✓ Timely Project Completion – Builders must stick to deadlines or pay compensation.

✓ Refunds & Compensation – Buyers can claim refunds if a project is delayed or abandoned.

✓ Escrow Accounts – Builders must keep 70% of funds in a secure account to prevent fund diversion.

How to File a Complaint Under RERA

1. Visit the State RERA Website (e.g., Maharashtra: maharera.mahaonline.gov.in).

2. Fill the Online Complaint Form with supporting documents.

3. Attend the Hearing at the RERA Tribunal.

4. Obtain Compensation or Refunds if the builder is found guilty.

✓ 2023 Update: 65% of RERA cases were resolved within 6 months, making it the fastest dispute resolution method for homebuyers.

2.5 Taxation & Stamp Duty: What Every Buyer Must Know

Buying a home involves multiple taxes, and miscalculating them can lead to financial stress.

Property Taxes & Registration Costs

Tax Type Rate

Stamp Duty 5-7% of property value (varies by state)

GST on Under-Construction Homes 5% (affordable housing) or 12% (luxury)

Capital Gains Tax (If Sold in <2 Years) 20% (Long Term) or Income Tax Slab Rate (Short Term)

✓ Tip: Buying a property jointly with a spouse can reduce stamp duty by 1-2% in some states.

Key Takeaways

✓ Verify all legal documents before making payments.

✓ Always check RERA registration to avoid fraudulent projects.

✓ Beware of hidden costs and misleading advertisements.

✓ Use digital verification tools to check land records and municipal approvals.

✓ File complaints under RERA for faster dispute resolution.

What's Next?

In Chapter 3: Financing Your Home Purchase, we will explore home loan strategies, EMI calculations, and tax-saving techniques to help you make an informed financial decision.

Did You Know?

The impact of iconic buildings on property values can be extraordinary. Take the Burj Khalifa in Dubai—the world's tallest building not only added $20 billion to Dubai's economy but also doubled property values in surrounding areas within just a decade. It's a powerful example of how landmark developments can transform entire neighborhoods.

III

Financing Your Home Purchase

"A smart loan strategy doesn't just fund your home—it builds generational wealth." — Financial Advisor

3.1 Why Smart Financial Planning is Essential

Buying a home isn't just about finding the right property—it's also about securing the right financing. Without proper planning, many homebuyers end up paying lakhs more in interest, taxes, and hidden fees than they should.

✓ *Did You Know?*

A   ₹50 lakh home loan at 8.5% for 20 years will cost you   ₹1.2 crore in total repayment. But with smart prepayments and refinancing, you can save up to   ₹25 lakh over time!

3.2 Home Loan Basics: Types, Interest Rates & Tenures

A home loan is the biggest financial commitment most people make, so it's essential to understand how it works.

Types of Home Loans in India

Loan Type

Best For

Interest Rate (2024)

Fixed-Rate Home Loan

Buyers who want stable EMIs

8.5% - 9.5%

Floating-Rate Home Loan

Buyers who want lower rates over time
8.2% - 8.8%
Balance Transfer Loan
Buyers who want to switch lenders for better rates
Varies
Pre-Approved Home Loan
Buyers who want faster processing
Slightly lower than standard loans
Loan Against Property
Self-employed individuals who need liquidity
9% - 12%
Home Construction Loan
People building their own home
8.5% - 10.5%
Pro Tip: Floating rates are ideal in a falling interest rate cycle, while fixed rates protect against rising rates.

3.3 Understanding EMIs & Reducing Interest Costs

Your Equated Monthly Installment (EMI) consists of principal repayment + interest.

EMI Calculation Formula

$$EMI = [P \times R \times (1+R)^N]/[(1+R)^N - 1]$$

Where:

- P = Loan Amount
- R = Monthly Interest Rate
- N = Loan Tenure (in months)

Example: EMI on ₹50 Lakh Loan

- Loan Tenure: 20 Years
- Interest Rate: 8.5%
- Monthly EMI: ₹43,391
- Total Repayment Over 20 Years: ₹1.04 Crore

✓ Smart EMI Reduction Strategies:

- Increase EMI by just 5% every year → Saves ₹10-15 lakh in interest.
- Make one extra EMI payment per year → Reduces tenure by 4-5 years.
- Use annual bonuses for prepayment → Directly reduces interest burden.

3.4 Hidden Charges & How to Avoid Them

Home loans come with many hidden charges that most buyers overlook.

Cost Breakdown of a ₹50 Lakh Home Loan

Charge Type

Amount

Processing Fee

₹10,000 - ₹50,000

Legal & Technical Charges

₹5,000 - ₹25,000

Loan Prepayment Charges

0% (for floating rate) to 2% (for fixed rate)

Late Payment Penalty

2% - 3% per month on overdue EMI

✓ Avoiding Hidden Costs:

? Compare lenders before applying—some banks waive processing fees for salaried professionals.

? Always read the fine print before signing any loan agreement.

3.5 Home Loan Tax Benefits: Save Lakhs Every Year

The Indian government offers multiple tax benefits on home loans, reducing your overall cost.

Breakdown of Home Loan Tax Benefits

Section

Purpose

Maximum Tax Deduction

Section 80C

Principal Repayment

₹1.5 Lakh per year

Section 24(b)

Interest Payment

₹2 Lakh per year

Section 80EE

First-Time Buyers

Additional ₹50,000

Section 80EEA

Affordable Housing (< ₹45L)

Additional ₹1.5 Lakh

✓ Example:

A person paying ₹2.5 lakh in home loan interest annually can claim a ₹2 lakh deduction, reducing tax liability by ₹40,000 per year (assuming 20% tax slab).

? Tip: Register the property jointly with a spouse to double tax benefits.

3.6 How to Choose the Right Lender

Not all home loans are equal. The right lender can save you lakhs over time.

Comparison of Top Lenders (2024)

Bank/NBFC	Interest Rate	Processing Fee	Prepayment Charges
SBI Home Loan	8.45%	₹10,000	Nil (floating)
HDFC Ltd	8.50%	₹10,000 - ₹25,000	Nil (floating)
ICICI Bank	8.55%	₹11,000 - ₹30,000	Nil (floating)
LIC Housing Finance	8.65%	₹10,000	2% (fixed rate)

? Choosing the Best Loan:

✓ Compare EMIs & processing fees before selecting a lender.

✓ Ask for pre-approved loan offers to get the lowest possible rate.

✓ Opt for balance transfers if your rate is higher than market rates.

3.7 The Balance Transfer Trick: Save Big on Interest

A home loan balance transfer allows you to switch to a lower-interest lender, reducing EMI and total interest paid.

Example: Balance Transfer Savings

· Existing Loan: ₹50 Lakh @ 9% for 20 Years

- New Loan Rate: 7.8% after 5 Years
- Total Savings: ₹6-8 Lakh in interest

✓ Tip: Balance transfers work best in the first 5-7 years of a loan.

3.8 Should You Rent or Buy?

For many buyers, renting can be cheaper than buying—depending on the city and market conditions.

Comparison: Buying vs. Renting a 2BHK in Bengaluru

Factor	Buying (₹1 Cr Flat)	Renting
Down Payment	₹20 Lakh	₹1 Lakh (Security)
EMI (8.5%)	₹80,000	₹30,000 Rent
Total Annual Cost	₹9.6 Lakh	₹3.6 Lakh
Appreciation Potential	₹10-15 Lakh (5 Years)	Zero

✓ Best Rule of Thumb:
- If the EMI is 3x higher than rent, renting is smarter.
- If property prices appreciate 8-10% annually, buying is better.

Key Takeaways

✓ Floating rate loans save more in falling interest cycles.

✓ Balance transfers can cut home loan interest by   ₹5-10 lakh.

✓ Prepayments & higher EMIs reduce total loan burden.

✓ Tax benefits can save up to   ₹5 lakh over time.

✓ Compare rent vs. buy before making a long-term commitment.

What's Next?

In Chapter 4: Choosing the Right Property, we'll explore how to evaluate locations, real estate appreciation, and resale value to make the best buying decision.

Did You Know?

Asia's oldest surviving property registry office still operates in Mumbai's Horniman Circle (formerly Elphinstone Circle), dating back to the 1860s. This historical institution has witnessed over 150 years of property transactions, serving as a testament to the importance of proper documentation in real estate.

IV

Choosing the Right Property

"Location, location, location—but also timing, due diligence, and a pinch of intuition." — Real Estate Expert

4.1 Why Choosing the Right Property Matters

Buying the wrong property can cost lakhs in financial losses, legal headaches, and resale difficulties. A smart buyer doesn't just focus on the builder's brochure—they analyze:

✓ Location Growth Potential – Is the area developing, or will prices stagnate?

✓ Builder Reputation – Has the developer delivered past projects on time?

✓ Legal & Infrastructure Status – Are there pending approvals or infrastructure issues?

✓ Rental Demand & Resale Value – Will you be able to sell or rent the property easily?

4.2 Understanding Location: The Most Important Factor
Golden Rule: The 3 E's of a Good Location

- Employment Hubs – Close to IT parks, business districts, or industrial areas.
- Education & Healthcare – Proximity to good schools, colleges, and hospitals.

• Expressways & Metro Connectivity – The better the transport network, the higher the property appreciation.

Case Study: Why Whitefield (Bengaluru) Became a Hotspot
• 1990s: Farmland, low development.
• 2000s: IT companies (TCS, Wipro) moved in, increasing demand.
• 2020s: Metro expansion → Prices increased 400% in 15 years.
✓ Lesson: Infrastructure projects can skyrocket property values in a few years.

4.3 Ready-to-Move vs. Under-Construction: Which is Better?

Factor
Ready-to-Move Property
Under-Construction Property

Cost
10-20% higher price
Cheaper (but carries risk)
Delivery Time
Immediate possession
Delays common (Check RERA)
GST Impact
No GST (saves 5-12%)
5% GST on base cost
Risk Factor
Low (legal approvals done)
High (project delays possible)
Investment Potential
Lower appreciation
Higher upside (if delivered on time)

Pro Tip: If buying under-construction, choose RERA-registered projects only.

4.4 Hidden Flaws: What to Check Before Buying

Most homebuyers only check brochure images and sample flats, but 70% of property issues aren't visible at first glance.

Checklist: How to Inspect a Property Like an Expert

Water & Drainage:
• Flush toilets during peak morning hours—low water pressure is a red flag.
• Check for seepage, damp walls, or mold—signs of poor construction.

Mobile Network & Internet Connectivity:
· Test network signal in bedrooms and basements.
· Check fiber broadband availability—slow internet lowers resale value.

Legal Approvals & Land Records:
· Verify occupancy certificate (OC) for ready properties.
· Cross-check land ownership details with sub-registrar records.

Builder's Reputation:
· Visit previous projects and ask residents about delays or issues.
· Check RERA complaints against the builder.

Noise & Pollution Levels:
· Visit at different times of the day to check for traffic noise or factory pollution nearby.

✓ Pro Tip: Visit during monsoon season to check for waterlogging issues.

4.5 Evaluating Resale & Rental Potential

How to Predict a Property's Future Value

✓ Annual Price Appreciation – If the area grows 8-10% per year, it's a strong market.

✓ Rental Yield – A good rental investment should provide 3-5% annual rental return.

✓ Upcoming Infrastructure Projects – Metro extensions, highways, and business parks increase property values.

Case Study: How a Buyer Earned   ₹50 Lakh in 5 Years

· 2018: Bought a 3BHK in Pune's Hinjewadi for   ₹80 lakh.
· 2023: Sold it for   ₹1.3 crore after metro expansion and IT growth.

✓ Lesson: Investing in high-growth corridors can double property value in a few years.

4.6 Avoiding Common Buying Mistakes

1. Buying Based on Hype
· Many buyers rush into projects because of flashy marketing.

✓ Reality Check: Always visit the site personally and verify approvals.

2. Ignoring Total Cost of Ownership
· Builders advertise   ₹60 lakh flats, but the final cost includes:

✓ Registration & stamp duty (5-7%)

✓ Maintenance fees

✓ Parking & club charges

3. Not Checking RERA Registration
· Unregistered projects can legally delay possession without penalty.

✓ Always buy RERA-approved projects to protect your investment.

Key Takeaways

✓ Location is the biggest factor in price appreciation.

✓ Ready-to-move saves GST, while under-construction offers better returns (if RERA-registered).

✓ Always check builder history & legal approvals before booking.

✓ Infrastructure projects increase property values significantly.

What's Next?

In Chapter 5: Negotiation & Deal Closing, we'll explore how to negotiate price reductions, get discounts, and secure the best deal with builders and sellers.

Did You Know?

The streets in the board game Monopoly weren't randomly chosen—they're based on real locations in Atlantic City, New Jersey. Interestingly, Baltic Avenue, the game's cheapest property, is now home to real estate worth over $1 million per unit. Talk about appreciation!

V

Negotiation & Deal Closing

"The quoted price is just the opening act—real magic happens in the negotiation."
— Mumbai's Top Property Broker

5.1 Why Negotiation is Essential in Real Estate

Many buyers assume that property prices are fixed, but in reality, almost every deal is negotiable. A well-negotiated deal can save you anywhere from ₹5 lakh to ₹50 lakh, depending on the property type and location.

✓ Did You Know?

· Builders have profit margins of 20-40%, which means they can offer discounts if pressured correctly.

· Festive season discounts can lower prices by 5-15%, but only if you negotiate smartly.

· Buyers who "walk away" from a deal often receive a call back within days with a better price.

5.2 Understanding Seller Psychology: How to Get a Lower Price

Different types of sellers have different motivations—and understanding this can give you a huge negotiation edge.

Types of Sellers & Best Negotiation Strategies

Seller Type

How to Negotiate

Builders (New Projects)

Ask for discounts, freebies, or better payment terms (builders need cash flow).

Investors (Resale Units)

Offer quick payment, point out market trends to justify a lower price.

Urgent Sellers (Financial Issues, Moving Abroad, Divorce, etc.)

Offer a faster transaction, use time pressure to get a better deal.

Long-Term Holders (No Urgency to Sell)

Be patient, follow up regularly, wait for price drops.

Pro Tip: A desperate seller is more flexible—look for properties where the owner needs a quick sale.

5.3 Effective Price Negotiation Strategies

1. The "Walk Away" Tactic

• If a builder refuses to lower the price, politely walk away.

• 60% of buyers get a call back within a week with a better offer.

2. The Comparative Market Trick

• Show data from nearby properties to prove that the price is too high.

• Example:

• "Sir, a similar 3BHK in the next tower is selling for ₹10 lakh less. Why should I pay more?"

3. The Bulk Buyer Approach

• If multiple buyers in a group negotiate together, builders offer better rates.

• Example: In 2023, a group of 10 IT professionals in Pune got ₹12 lakh discounts per flat by booking together.

4. The Festival Season Hack

• Builders desperately push sales during Diwali, Navratri, and New Year.

• Negotiate extra freebies like modular kitchens, parking, and zero-floor-rise charges.

5. The "I'm Paying in Cash" Trick (Legal & Bank Approved)

• Offer a higher upfront payment (e.g., 30-40%) to get a lower price.

• This works well with investors and resale properties.

Pro Tip: Always ask for more than you expect—the seller will meet you halfway.

5.4 Understanding "Discounts" vs. "Hidden Costs"

Some builders inflate the base price before offering a "discount." Learn to calculate the real price.

Common Builder Tricks & How to Counter Them

Builder Trick

Reality Check

"Prices will increase next month!"

False: This is a common sales pressure tactic.

"Limited period offer: ₹10 lakh discount!"

Verify the actual pre-discount price before believing it.

"Free modular kitchen & parking!"

Check if these costs were already added to the price.

Pro Tip: Always compare the "discounted price" with recent sales in the same building.

5.5 Negotiating Builder Payment Plans

Builders offer different payment schemes, but not all are good for buyers.

Comparison of Payment Plans

Plan Type

Pros

Cons

Construction-Linked Plan

Pay in stages, less financial risk

Delays = More EMI burden

Subvention Plan (No EMI till possession)

No financial burden till handover

Higher base price (hidden cost)

Down Payment Plan (80-90% upfront)

Best for big discounts

High financial risk if project is delayed

Pro Tip: Always read the fine print—some subvention plans shift EMI burden to buyers later.

5.6 Closing the Deal: Legal & Financial Safeguards

1. Token Amount & Sale Agreement

• Builders demand   ₹1-5 lakh as a token amount—but what happens if you back out?

• Check refund policy before paying anything.

2. Verify All Costs in Writing

• Builders often add extra charges later (maintenance fees, club membership, etc.).

• Demand a written breakdown of all costs before signing the agreement.

3. Home Loan Finalization

• Get your home loan pre-approved to negotiate a better deal.

• Compare loan offers from multiple banks/NBFCs before committing.

4. Sale Agreement & Possession Date

· Include penalty clauses—if the builder delays possession, they should pay compensation.

· Example: " ₹5,000 per month penalty if possession is delayed beyond X date."

Pro Tip: Get all agreements checked by a real estate lawyer before signing.

5.7 Case Study: How a Buyer Saved ₹15 Lakh in a Deal

Case:

· Rahul, an IT professional in Bengaluru, was buying a ₹1.2 crore apartment.

· The builder initially refused discounts, claiming "fixed pricing."

How He Negotiated Smartly:

✔ Showed lower-priced resale listings in the same project.

✔ Waited until December (low sales period) and revisited.

✔ Paid 40% upfront to secure a better deal.

✔ Asked for zero floor-rise charges + free clubhouse membership.

✔ Final Savings: ₹15 lakh reduced price + freebies worth ₹3 lakh.

Key Takeaways

✔ Never accept the first price—everything in real estate is negotiable.

✔ Use market data & competition to justify lower prices.

✔ Festive seasons & bulk buying can help get bigger discounts.

✔ Always verify builder offers & hidden costs before signing.

✔ Legal agreements should include refund clauses & penalty terms.

What's Next?

In Chapter 6: Home Loans & Tax Planning, we'll explore advanced mortgage strategies, tax-saving tips, and government schemes to reduce home loan costs.

Did You Know?

The term "real estate" has fascinating etymological roots. The word "real" comes from the Latin "res," meaning "thing." It was originally used to distinguish physical property (called "real") from personal property (called "chattel")—a distinction that remains important in property law today.

VI

Home Loans & Tax Planning

"A smart loan strategy doesn't just finance your home—it builds your financial future." — Banking Expert

6.1 Why Smart Home Loan Planning Matters

For most homebuyers, a home loan is the largest financial commitment of their lives. A bad loan decision can cost you lakhs in extra interest, while a smart loan strategy can help you save ₹10-25 lakh over time.

✔ Did You Know?

· A ₹50 lakh home loan at 8.5% for 20 years costs ₹1.2 crore in total repayment.

· But with smart prepayments and balance transfers, you can reduce this by ₹20 lakh or more.

6.2 Understanding Home Loan Types & Choosing the Right One

Different types of home loans are suited for different buyers.

Comparison of Home Loan Types

Loan Type

Best For

Interest Rate (2024)

Fixed-Rate Home Loan

Buyers who want stable EMIs

8.5% - 9.5%

Floating-Rate Home Loan

Buyers who want lower rates over time

8.2% - 8.8%

Balance Transfer Loan

Buyers looking to switch lenders for lower rates

Varies

Pre-Approved Home Loan

Buyers who want faster processing

Slightly lower than standard loans

Home Construction Loan

Those building their own home

8.5% - 10.5%

Pro Tip: Floating rates work best in falling interest cycles, while fixed rates protect against sudden hikes.

6.3 How to Reduce EMI & Save Lakhs on Interest

Your Equated Monthly Installment (EMI) consists of principal repayment + interest.

EMI Calculation Formula

EMI = = $[P \times R \times (1+R)^N]/[(1+R)^N-1]$

$$[P \times R \times (1+R)^N]/[(1+R)^N - 1]$$

Where:

· P = Loan Amount

· R = Monthly Interest Rate

· N = Loan Tenure (in months)

Example: EMI on ₹50 Lakh Loan at 8.5% Interest

· Loan Tenure: 20 Years

· Monthly EMI: ₹43,391

· Total Repayment Over 20 Years: ₹1.04 Crore

Smart Strategies to Reduce EMI Burden

✓ Increase EMI by just 5% every year → Saves ₹10-15 lakh in interest.

✓ Make one extra EMI payment per year → Reduces tenure by 4-5 years.

✓ Use bonuses for prepayment → Directly reduces interest burden.

6.4 Home Loan Hidden Costs & How to Avoid Them

Many buyers focus on interest rates but forget about hidden charges.

Charge Type

Amount

Processing Fee

₹10,000 - ₹50,000

Legal & Technical Charges

₹5,000 -   ₹25,000

Loan Prepayment Charges

0% (for floating rate) to 2% (for fixed rate)

Late Payment Penalty

2-3% per month on overdue EMI

✓ Avoiding Hidden Costs:

? Compare lenders before applying—some banks waive processing fees.

? Always read the fine print before signing any loan agreement.

6.5 Home Loan Tax Benefits: How to Save   ₹5+ Lakh in Taxes

The Indian government offers multiple tax benefits to reduce home loan costs.

Breakdown of Home Loan Tax Benefits

Tax Section

Purpose

Maximum Deduction

Section 80C

Principal Repayment

₹1.5 Lakh per year

Section 24(b)

Interest Payment

₹2 Lakh per year

Section 80EE

First-Time Buyers

Additional   ₹50,000

Section 80EEA

Affordable Housing (<   ₹45L)

Additional   ₹1.5 Lakh

Example: How a Buyer Saves on Taxes

· Loan Amount: ₹40 Lakh

· Annual Interest Paid: ₹2.5 Lakh

· Tax Deduction Used:

✓   ₹2 Lakh deduction under Section 24(b)

✓   ₹50,000 deduction under Section 80EE

✓ Total Savings: ₹40,000 per year (assuming a 20% tax slab).

Pro Tip: Register the property jointly with a spouse to double tax benefits.

6.6 Home Loan Balance Transfer: Save   ₹5-10 Lakh Easily

A home loan balance transfer allows you to switch to a lower-interest lender, reducing EMI and total interest paid.

Example: Balance Transfer Savings

· Existing Loan: ₹50 Lakh @ 9% for 20 Years

· New Loan Rate: 7.8% after 5 Years

· Total Savings: ₹6-8 Lakh in interest

✓ Tip: Balance transfers work best in the first 5-7 years of a loan.

6.7 Should You Buy or Rent?

Many homebuyers debate whether renting or buying is smarter.

Comparison: Buying vs. Renting a 2BHK in Bengaluru

Factor	Buying (₹1 Cr Flat)	Renting
Down Payment	₹20 Lakh	₹1 Lakh (Security)
EMI (8.5%)	₹80,000	₹30,000 Rent
Total Annual Cost	₹9.6 Lakh	₹3.6 Lakh
Appreciation Potential	₹10-15 Lakh (5 Years)	Zero

✓ Rule of Thumb:

· If the EMI is 3x higher than rent, renting is smarter.

· If property prices appreciate 8-10% annually, buying is better.

Key Takeaways

✓ Floating rate loans save more in falling interest cycles.

✓ Balance transfers can cut home loan interest by   ₹5-10 lakh.

✓ Prepayments & higher EMIs reduce total loan burden.

✓ Tax benefits can save up to   ₹5 lakh over time.

✓ Compare rent vs. buy before making a long-term commitment.

What's Next?

In Chapter 7: The Indian Real Estate Industry Overview, we'll explore career opportunities, investment trends, and the future of the sector.

Did You Know?

Color psychology plays a crucial role in real estate sales. According to Zillow research, homes painted white or in neutral colors sell 10% faster on average than those with bold color schemes. Buyers tend to associate these colors with cleanliness and modernity.

VII
The Indian Real Estate Industry Overview

"Real estate isn't just about buildings—it's about the economy, careers, and future growth." — Industry Expert

7.1 Understanding India's Real Estate Sector

India's real estate industry is one of the largest contributors to the GDP, projected to reach $1 trillion by 2030 and contribute 13% to the GDP by 2025.

✓ *Did You Know?*

· *India has over 75 million homebuyers annually, making it one of the world's fastest-growing property markets.*

· *65% of India's wealth is stored in real estate, making it the preferred investment choice for most Indians.*

7.2 Key Segments of the Indian Real Estate Market

1. Residential Real Estate

✓ Demand driven by urbanization & rising incomes.

✓ Affordable housing dominates—PMAY has created 1.2 crore new homebuyers.

✓ Luxury housing is booming in Mumbai, Delhi, Bengaluru, and Hyderabad.

2. Commercial Real Estate

✓ Office spaces in Gurugram, Bengaluru, and Pune have seen 40% rental growth in 5 years.

✓ Co-working spaces & hybrid offices are growing post-pandemic.

✓ Foreign investors are pouring money into Grade A office spaces.

3. Retail & Mall Spaces

✓ India's retail real estate will grow $100 billion by 2030.

✓ Shopping malls are shifting towards experience-driven spaces (entertainment, food courts).

4. Industrial & Warehousing

✓ E-commerce boom (Amazon, Flipkart) is driving logistics & warehouse expansion.

✓ Delhi NCR & Mumbai are emerging as top warehousing hubs.

5. PropTech & Smart Cities

✓ AI & blockchain are transforming real estate transactions.

✓ India is developing 100 Smart Cities—Dholera & GIFT City are top examples.

Pro Tip: Investors should focus on emerging commercial & warehousing markets for high returns.

7.3 Government Policies & Real Estate Growth

1. RERA (2016): Boosting Transparency

✓ Ensures timely project delivery.

✓ 70% of funds must be in escrow accounts to prevent fraud.

2. REITs: Making Commercial Real Estate Accessible

✓ Real Estate Investment Trusts allow small investors to own shares in office properties.

✓ India's first REIT (Embassy Office Parks) gave 15%+ annual returns since 2019.

3. FDI & Foreign Investments

✓ 100% FDI allowed in real estate development.

✓ $50 billion+ foreign investments since 2015.

✓ Impact: More global money = better infrastructure, modern buildings, and higher job creation.

7.4 Real Estate Careers: High-Growth Job Opportunities

The Indian real estate industry employs over 52 million people across various roles.

Top Career Options in Real Estate

Career Path

Avg Salary (₹ per year)

Growth Potential

Real Estate Agent

₹3L -   ₹20L

High (Unlimited commissions)
Property Valuer
₹4L - ₹12L
Moderate
Real Estate Lawyer
₹5L - ₹25L
High
PropTech Developer
₹6L - ₹30L
Very High
Construction Manager
₹7L - ₹25L
High

✓ Tip: The best-paying careers are in luxury real estate, commercial brokerage, and PropTech startups.

7.5 Future of Indian Real Estate (2025-2035)

✓ Tier-2 & Tier-3 cities will drive 50% of real estate demand.

✓ AI & blockchain will streamline property transactions & reduce fraud.

✓ Sustainable & smart homes will become mainstream demand.

✓ Hybrid work models will reshape commercial real estate.

Key Takeaways

✓ India's real estate market is set to reach $1 trillion by 2030.

✓ RERA & REITs have increased transparency & investor participation.

✓ Careers in real estate can be highly lucrative, especially in PropTech & commercial brokerage.

✓ Sustainable & smart homes will define the next decade.

What's Next?

In Chapter 8: Real Estate Investment Strategies, we'll explore rental income, flipping properties, land investments, and REITs to maximize returns.

Did You Know?

The Vatican City, while being the world's smallest country at just 109 acres, maintains its own unique real estate market. Through centuries-old treaties, it owns approximately 12% of Rome's land, making it one of the world's most concentrated property owners.

VIII
Real Estate Investment Strategies

"Real estate is the closest thing to a guaranteed wealth-building tool—if you know how to play the game right." — Investment Expert

8.1 Why Invest in Real Estate?

Real estate investment offers three powerful benefits:

✓ Appreciation: Property values typically increase over time, creating long-term wealth.

✓ Rental Income: Generates passive cash flow, covering EMIs and expenses.

✓ Leverage: Unlike stocks, you can buy real estate with just 20-30% down payment and use a loan for the rest.

✓ *Did You Know?*

· Indian real estate has delivered 12-15% annualized returns in metro cities over the last decade.

· Rental yields range from 3-5% in residential and 6-10% in commercial properties.

8.2 Types of Real Estate Investments & Their Returns

1. Residential Property Investment

✓ Ideal for long-term appreciation.

✓ Suitable for first-time investors.

✓ Rental yield: 2.5% - 4% per year.

✓ Appreciation potential: 5-10% per year in Tier-1 cities.

Pro Tip: Invest in ready-to-move properties to avoid construction delays.

2. Commercial Real Estate (Office Spaces, Shops, Warehouses)

✓ Generates higher rental income than residential.

✓ Demand driven by IT parks, co-working spaces, retail hubs.

✓ Rental yield: 6-10% per year.

✓ Appreciation potential: 8-12% per year.

✓ *Case Study: How an Investor Earned ₹50 Lakh in 5 Years*

· *2018: Purchased a 500 sq. ft. office space in Pune for ₹80 lakh.*

· *2023: Rented it out at ₹50,000 per month (7.5% rental yield).*

· *Resold in 2023 for ₹1.3 crore → ₹50 lakh profit.*

3. Land Investments (Plots, Farmland, Undeveloped Land)

✓ High appreciation potential (15-20% per year in emerging areas).

✓ Ideal for long-term investors willing to wait for city expansion.

✓ Risk: No rental income unless converted into housing/commercial use.

Pro Tip: Buy land near proposed highways, metro lines, or industrial zones for maximum appreciation.

4. REITs (Real Estate Investment Trusts)

✓ Best for small investors (minimum ₹10,000 investment).

✓ Invests in office buildings, malls, and hotels.

✓ Provides regular dividend income + capital appreciation.

✓ Best Performing REIT in India: Embassy Office Parks – 15%+ annual returns since 2019.

Pro Tip: REITs offer higher liquidity than physical real estate—ideal for first-time investors.

8.3 Rental Income Strategies

How to Choose a High-Rental Yield Property

✓ Near business hubs & IT parks → Strong tenant demand.

✓ Furnished homes → Higher rent & faster occupancy.

✓ Metro-connected locations → 15-25% higher rental value.

How to Maximize Rental Returns

✓ Rent agreements should include a 5-10% annual rent escalation clause.

✓ List properties on multiple platforms (99acres, MagicBricks, Airbnb) for higher occupancy.

✓ Offer flexible lease terms to attract corporate tenants.

Pro Tip: NRIs & corporate tenants pay higher rents & are long-term tenants.

8.4 Flipping Properties for Profit (Buy-Improve-Sell Strategy)

Flipping involves buying undervalued properties, renovating, and selling for a profit.

Best Properties to Flip

✓ Old apartments in high-demand localities.

✓ Bank auctioned properties (often 15-30% below market rate).

✓ Distressed sales (owners needing urgent cash).

Pro Tip: Focus on low-cost renovations (paint, lighting, modern kitchens) that increase value without excessive costs.

8.5 How to Identify Emerging Investment Hotspots

5 Signs of a High-Growth Location

✓ Metro, airport, or highway expansion.

✓ Large corporate investments (factories, IT parks).

✓ Rising rental demand & low vacancy rates.

✓ Government incentives for real estate projects.

✓ RERA-registered projects with top builders.

Hot Investment Locations (2025-2030)

• Pune (Hinjewadi, Baner) – IT & startup hub.

• Hyderabad (Kokapet, Tellapur) – Fastest-growing metro city.

• Delhi NCR (Noida Expressway, Dwarka Expressway) – New infra projects.

• Chennai (OMR, Porur) – High rental demand.

• Bengaluru (Sarjapur Road, Devanahalli) – Strong IT & commercial growth.

Pro Tip: Pre-launch bookings often offer 10-20% lower prices than post-launch sales.

8.6 Managing Risks in Real Estate Investing

Common Risks & How to Avoid Them

Risk

Prevention Strategy

Delayed Possession

Buy ready-to-move or RERA-registered projects.

Low Rental Demand

Research tenant demand before investing.

Legal Issues

Verify land titles, builder reputation & approvals.

Market Fluctuations

Invest for the long term (5-10 years).

Pro Tip: Always keep 6-12 months of emergency funds for loan EMIs & maintenance costs.

Key Takeaways

✓ Real estate investment offers appreciation, rental income, and wealth creation.

✓ Commercial real estate & REITs provide higher rental returns than residential.

✓ Flipping properties & pre-launch deals offer high short-term gains.

✓ Always choose RERA-approved projects to avoid legal risks.

✓ Emerging cities & infrastructure projects are top growth areas for the next decade.

What's Next?

In Chapter 9: The Future of Real Estate in India, we'll explore AI, blockchain, smart cities, co-living spaces, and how technology is reshaping the real estate sector.

Did You Know?

Not all real estate appreciates over time. In Japan, most residential properties are considered disposable, losing value over time due to strict earthquake codes and cultural preferences. The typical lifespan of a Japanese home is just 30 years before demolition—a stark contrast to Western real estate markets.

IX

The Future of Real Estate in India

"The real estate industry is on the verge of a technology revolution—investors who adapt will lead the future." — PropTech CEO

9.1 The Changing Landscape of Real Estate

The Indian real estate market is undergoing a major transformation driven by:

✓ Technology (PropTech, AI, blockchain, digital transactions).

✓ Sustainability (Green buildings, energy-efficient homes).

✓ Changing demographics (Co-living, flexible workspaces, urban migration).

✓ *Did You Know?*

·*Over $1 billion has been invested in PropTech startups in India since 2020.*

·*India aims to develop 100 Smart Cities by 2040, creating a new era of real estate development.*

9.2 PropTech: The AI & Blockchain Revolution in Real Estate

How AI is Changing Real Estate

✓ AI-powered price predictions → Helps investors buy at the right time.

✓ Virtual reality (VR) property tours → Buyers can see homes remotely.

✓ Chatbots & AI agents → Automate property transactions & documentation.

✓ Example: NoBroker uses AI for rent pricing & tenant matchmaking, reducing broker dependence.

Blockchain: The Future of Secure Real Estate Transactions

✔ Smart contracts will eliminate fraud & middlemen.

✔ Property titles on blockchain → Instant verification of land ownership.

✔ Tokenization of real estate → Allows fractional ownership of big properties.

Example: India's first blockchain-based land registry pilot launched in Telangana in 2022.

Pro Tip: Investing early in PropTech startups or AI-driven real estate funds can yield massive returns.

9.3 Smart Cities: The Next Billion-Dollar Investment Opportunity

What Defines a Smart City?

✔ AI-powered traffic & infrastructure management.

✔ Sustainable urban planning (green buildings, solar energy).

✔ Seamless digital governance (e-registration, online municipal services).

Top Smart City Projects in India

• Dholera, Gujarat – India's first planned smart city (₹1 lakh crore investment).

• GIFT City, Gujarat – India's global financial hub.

• Navi Mumbai Airport Influence Zone (NAINA) – Next big real estate hotspot.

Pro Tip: Investing near Smart City projects can deliver 20-30% returns in 5-7 years.

9.4 Co-Living & Flexible Workspaces: The Future of Housing & Offices

✔ Co-living spaces (like Zolo, Stanza Living) offer flexible, fully managed rental homes.

✔ Hybrid work models are reducing demand for traditional office spaces but increasing demand for co-working hubs.

✔ Real estate developers are now designing homes with built-in office spaces for remote workers.

✔ Investment Tip: Co-living spaces generate 15-20% higher rental returns than traditional rentals.

9.5 Green Buildings & Sustainability: The Future of Housing

✔ Green-certified buildings sell for 5-10% higher prices.

✔ Buyers prefer solar panels, energy-efficient designs, and rainwater harvesting.

✔ Government incentives for sustainable housing are increasing.

Pro Tip: Investing in LEED-certified properties can boost resale value & reduce maintenance costs.

9.6 Future Investment Hotspots: Where to Invest in 2030 & Beyond

Emerging Investment Locations

✓ Hyderabad's Pharma City – Next IT & biotech hub.

✓ Chennai's OMR Expansion – Fastest-growing tech corridor.

✓ Bengaluru's Devanahalli (Near Airport) – Strongest infrastructure growth.

✓ Pune's Hinjewadi & Mahalunge – IT-driven real estate boom.

Pro Tip: Invest early in Tier-2 cities with strong infrastructure growth—these areas will outperform metros in price appreciation.

Key Takeaways

✓ PropTech & AI will revolutionize property buying & investing.

✓ Blockchain-based land registries will reduce fraud & delays.

✓ Smart cities & sustainable buildings will define future urban development.

✓ Co-living spaces & remote work hubs are the next big real estate opportunities.

✓ Investing in high-growth Tier-2 cities offers the best long-term appreciation.

What's Next?

In Chapter 10: Mastering Real Estate Negotiation & Deal Structuring, we'll explore advanced negotiation techniques, deal structuring hacks, and how to get the best financing terms.

Did You Know?

The 2008 U.S. housing crisis led to the repossession of 7.5 million homes—enough to house Switzerland's entire population. This staggering figure illustrates the unprecedented scale of the crisis and its impact on countless families.

X

Mastering Real Estate Negotiation & Deal Structuring

"The best real estate investors don't just find great deals—they create them." — *Investment Expert*

10.1 Why Negotiation & Deal Structuring Matter

The difference between a good deal and a great deal is often in the negotiation and structuring of the transaction. Even a 5% reduction in price or better financing terms can save lakhs over the long term.

✓ *Did You Know?*

· *Buyers who negotiate effectively save ₹5-20 lakh on average per property.*

· *Flexible financing structures can help investors buy without using all their savings.*

· *Some sellers are willing to offer hidden discounts, extended payment plans, or lease-back options—but only if you know how to ask.*

10.2 Advanced Negotiation Tactics: Getting the Best Price

1. The "Walk-Away" Strategy

✓ If a builder or seller refuses to lower the price, politely walk away.

✓ 80% of buyers who walk away get a call back with a better deal.

2. The "Multiple Offers" Tactic

✓ Get quotes from at least 3-4 builders or sellers.

✓ Use the lowest offer as leverage to negotiate others down.

3. The "End-of-Quarter" & Festive Discount Hack

✓ Builders offer bigger discounts at the end of financial quarters (March, June, Sept, Dec).

✓ Festive seasons (Diwali, Dussehra) bring 5-15% price cuts and zero-cost add-ons (modular kitchen, parking, floor rise waiver).

4. The "Delayed Payment" Trick (Only for Investors)

✓ Negotiate for extended payment plans → Helps avoid taking a loan immediately.

✓ Works best for under-construction projects where builders need cash flow.

Pro Tip: If a builder is struggling to meet sales targets, they may agree to lower down payments or EMI holidays.

10.3 Creative Deal Structuring for Maximum Profit

A smart investor doesn't just negotiate price—they structure the deal to minimize risk and maximize gains.

1. Lease Option (Rent-to-Own) Strategy (Best for Investors & First-Time Buyers)

✓ Negotiate a rent-to-own contract → Pay rent now, with an option to buy later at today's price.

✓ Useful when property prices are expected to rise but you need time to arrange finances.

Example: In 2019, an investor in Mumbai locked in a rent-to-own deal for ₹1 crore, paid rent for 2 years, and later exercised the purchase option when market prices shot up to ₹1.3 crore—gaining ₹30 lakh in equity without upfront capital investment.

2. Seller Financing (Zero Bank Loan Strategy)

✓ Instead of a bank loan, convince the seller to finance part of the property cost.

✓ Ideal when buying from investors or NRI sellers who don't need immediate full payment.

✓ Benefits: No bank EMI, flexible repayment terms, lower cost.

Example: Buyer purchases a ₹1 crore property, pays ₹50 lakh upfront, and negotiates a 0% EMI deal with the seller for the remaining ₹ 50 lakh over 5 years.

3. Joint Venture (JV) Deals for Land Investors

✓ Find a landowner → Propose a profit-sharing model where you develop the land together.

✓ Works well for investors with strong real estate contacts but limited capital.

Pro Tip: Always draft a legally binding JV agreement to avoid disputes.

10.4 Financing Hacks: Reducing Interest & Loan Costs

Most homebuyers and investors focus on getting a loan, but few focus on structuring it correctly to save lakhs.

How to Reduce Home Loan Burden

Strategy

Savings Potential

Increase EMI by 5% every year

Saves   ₹10-15 lakh over 20 years

Make one extra EMI payment per year

Cuts loan tenure by 4-5 years

Refinance if interest rates drop by 1%+

Saves   ₹5-10 lakh

Use bonuses/tax refunds for prepayments

Lowers total interest cost

Pro Tip: Banks don't tell you this, but small prepayments in the first 5 years of a loan save the most money on interest.

10.5 The Hidden Costs of a Real Estate Deal & How to Avoid Them

Many buyers focus only on the property price, but there are hidden costs that can significantly impact your budget.

Hidden Charges to Watch Out For

Cost Type

Typical Amount

Stamp Duty & Registration

5-7% of property value

Floor Rise Charges

₹50-   ₹200 per sq. ft. for higher floors

Maintenance Charges (Advance)

₹2-5 per sq. ft.

Parking & Club Membership

₹2-10 lakh (one-time fee)

Pro Tip: Always ask for a detailed cost breakup in writing before signing any agreement.

10.6 Case Study: How an Investor Bought a   ₹2 Crore Property for   ₹ 1.6 Crore

Case Details:

· Buyer wanted a luxury 3BHK in Gurgaon.

· Builder initially quoted ₹2 crore (all-inclusive price).

Negotiation & Structuring Strategy:

✓ Researched unsold inventory in the same project → Found out that the builder had excess stock.

✓ Used the "Walk-Away" strategy → Builder called back within a week.

✓ Requested zero-cost add-ons (₹10 lakh worth of upgrades).

✓ Opted for a 40% upfront payment → Negotiated a bulk discount.

✓ Final Deal: ₹1.6 crore (₹40 lakh saved) + ₹10 lakh worth of freebies.

Key Takeaways

✓ Everything is negotiable—buyers who ask for discounts save lakhs.

✓ Creative financing (seller financing, JV deals) reduces upfront capital needs.

✓ Smart EMI strategies & prepayments cut loan costs by ₹5-20 lakh.

✓ Hidden charges like floor rise & club membership can add 5-10% to costs—always verify before signing.

✓ Real estate investors who structure deals creatively earn higher returns with lower risks.

What's Next?

In Chapter 11: Legal Framework & Consumer Protection, we'll cover RERA laws, homebuyer rights, property disputes, and how to legally safeguard your investment.

Did You Know?

India's housing landscape is rapidly evolving, with over 15,000 gated communities nationwide. Bengaluru leads this trend, as young professionals increasingly prioritize security and lifestyle amenities in their housing choices.

XI

Legal Framework & Consumer Protection

"Knowing your legal rights in real estate is not optional—it's essential." — Property Law Expert

11.1 Why Legal Protection is Critical in Real Estate

Many homebuyers and investors face fraud, delays, and legal disputes due to:

✓ Unethical builders violating RERA guidelines.

✓ Delayed possession or abandoned projects.

✓ Disputes over title ownership and encumbrances.

Did You Know?

· Over 40% of real estate disputes in India involve project delays.

· RERA has helped resolve   ₹1 lakh crore+ worth of disputes since 2017.

11.2 Understanding RERA: The Game-Changer for Homebuyers

The Real Estate (Regulation and Development) Act (2016) was introduced to protect buyers and enforce transparency.

Key Provisions of RERA

✓ Mandatory Registration → All projects over 500 sq. meters or 8 apartments must be RERA-registered.

✓ Escrow Account for Builders → 70% of buyer funds must be kept in a separate account to prevent fund diversion.

✓ Timely Possession → Developers must provide a definite completion date.

✓ Full Disclosure → Builders must publish project details, approvals, and financials on the RERA website.

✓ Compensation for Delays → Homebuyers can claim refunds with interest if possession is delayed.

Pro Tip: Always check if a project is RERA-registered on the state RERA website before booking.

11.3 How to File a Complaint Under RERA & Get Compensation

If a builder violates RERA regulations, you can file a complaint for refund or compensation.

Step-by-Step Guide to Filing a RERA Complaint

- Visit the State RERA Website (e.g., Maharashtra: maharera.mahaonline.gov.in).
- Fill the Complaint Form – Provide project details, issue, and builder information.
- Attach Supporting Documents – Sale agreement, payment receipts, builder communication.
- Pay the Filing Fee (₹1,000 - ₹5,000, varies by state).
- Attend the RERA Hearing – Present your case before the tribunal.

Timeframe for Resolution: Most RERA cases are resolved within 3-6 months.

11.4 Common Real Estate Frauds & How to Avoid Them

1. Delayed Possession & Stalled Projects

✓ Solution: Only invest in RERA-registered projects and check builder history.

2. Selling Without Clear Land Title

✓ Solution: Verify title deeds & encumbrance certificate from the Sub-Registrar's Office.

3. Fake Promises & Misleading Advertisements

✓ Solution: Demand everything in writing in the sale agreement before booking.

4. Illegal Construction & Unauthorized Projects

✓ Solution: Check project approvals on municipal or RERA portals.

Pro Tip: Never pay 100% upfront before project completion—only pay in stages as per RERA guidelines.

11.5 How to Resolve Property Disputes

If you face title issues, builder fraud, or illegal charges, you have multiple legal remedies.

Legal Avenues for Property Disputes

Dispute Type
Where to File a Complaint
Timeframe

Project Delay / Fraud
RERA Tribunal
3-6 Months
Land Title Dispute
Civil Court
1-5 Years
Overcharging by Builder
Consumer Court
6-12 Months
Illegal Construction
Municipal Authority
Varies

Pro Tip: RERA is the fastest dispute resolution mechanism for homebuyers.

11.6 Understanding Stamp Duty, Registration & Legal Costs

When buying a property, legal charges can add 5-8% to the total cost.

Breakdown of Legal Costs

Charge Type
Typical Amount

Stamp Duty
5-7% of property value (varies by state)
Registration Fee
1% of property value
Legal Fees for Documentation
₹10,000 - ₹50,000
Mutation Charges (Updating Ownership in Govt. Records)
₹5,000 - ₹25,000

Pro Tip: Women buyers get 1-2% stamp duty discount in some states.

11.7 Case Study: How a Buyer Won a ₹25 Lakh Refund Under RERA

Case:

· Buyer purchased a ₹1.5 crore apartment in Gurugram in 2018.

· Builder delayed possession by 3 years without explanation.

Legal Steps Taken:

✓ Filed a RERA complaint with all supporting documents.

✓ Attended 3 RERA hearings over 5 months.

✓ Won a   ₹25 lakh refund + 9% interest per annum.

✓ Lesson: RERA is a powerful tool for buyers facing fraud or delays.

Key Takeaways

✓ Always check RERA registration before investing in any property.

✓ Use RERA & Consumer Court to resolve builder disputes quickly.

✓ Verify all land titles & approvals to avoid legal issues.

✓ Understand stamp duty, registration fees & hidden legal costs.

✓ Legal knowledge protects buyers from fraud & financial loss.

What's Next?

In Chapter 12: The Complete Home Buying Checklist, we'll cover step-by-step guides, financial planning, legal verification, and finalizing the best property deal.

Did You Know?

The Empire State Building's construction was a marvel of efficiency, completed in just 410 days (1930-1931). Even more impressive, it achieved profitability from its observation deck alone within six months of opening—proving that innovative revenue streams can make or break commercial properties.

XII

The Complete Home Buying Checklist

"Buying a home isn't just about finding the right property—it's about making the right decision at every step." — *Real Estate Advisor*

12.1 Why a Home Buying Checklist is Essential

Buying a home is one of the biggest financial decisions you'll make. Missing even one critical step can lead to legal disputes, unexpected costs, or poor investment choices.

Did You Know?

·65% of homebuyers in India regret not researching builder credibility before purchasing.

·25% of buyers face legal issues due to missing property documentation.

This checklist ensures that you make a fully informed, risk-free purchase.

12.2 Step 1: Financial Planning & Budgeting

1. Calculate How Much You Can Afford

✓ Home Loan Eligibility = 40-50% of your monthly income.

✓ Down Payment = 15-30% of property cost.

✓ Hidden Costs (Stamp duty, registration, maintenance fees) = 5-8% extra.

Pro Tip: Your monthly EMI should not exceed 30-40% of your net income for financial stability.

2. Check Your Credit Score (Before Applying for a Loan)

✓ 750+ score = Best interest rates.

✓ Below 650? Pay off debts before applying.

12.3 Step 2: Choosing the Right Property

✓ Location Matters:

· Near IT hubs, metros, highways, hospitals, and schools.

· Check crime rates & future infrastructure projects.

✓ Property Type:

· Ready-to-move: No GST, immediate possession.

· Under-construction: Cheaper, but only buy RERA-registered projects.

✓ Builder Reputation:

· Visit previous projects.

· Check RERA website for complaints & project delays.

Pro Tip: Visit the property at night and during monsoon to check for noise, waterlogging, and traffic conditions.

12.4 Step 3: Legal Verification & Due Diligence

✓ Check These Legal Documents:

? Title Deed & Encumbrance Certificate (Ensure clear ownership).

? RERA Registration Certificate (Verify project status).

? Sale Agreement (Verify price, payment schedule, penalty clauses).

? Occupancy & Completion Certificates (For ready properties).

Pro Tip: Hire a real estate lawyer to verify documents—costs ₹10,000-₹30,000 but can save lakhs in legal disputes.

12.5 Step 4: Negotiation & Price Finalization

✓ Negotiate the Base Price & Hidden Costs:

? Ask for 10-15% discount on quoted price.

? Get freebies (parking, modular kitchen, waiver of floor-rise charges).

? Compare multiple properties before committing.

Pro Tip: Builders offer the biggest discounts at the end of the financial quarter & during festive seasons.

12.6 Step 5: Home Loan Processing

✓ Compare Home Loan Offers from Multiple Banks:

? Check interest rates, processing fees, and prepayment penalties.

? Apply for a pre-approved loan for faster processing.

Pro Tip: Choose floating rate loans when interest rates are falling & fixed-rate loans when rates are rising.

12.7 Step 6: Finalizing the Sale Agreement & Registration

✓ Before Signing the Agreement:

? Check payment schedule & penalty clauses for delay.

? Ensure all amenities & commitments are in writing.

✓ Property Registration Process:

?Pay stamp duty & registration fees (5-7% of property cost).

?Register the property at the Sub-Registrar's Office.

?Get the Sale Deed & Mutation Certificate (updates government records).

Pro Tip: Women buyers get 1-2% lower stamp duty in many states—buy jointly for tax benefits.

12.8 Step 7: Moving In & Post-Purchase Checklist

✓ Check the Apartment & Society Rules:

? Confirm maintenance fees & water supply schedules.

? Register with the Resident Welfare Association (RWA).

? Set up utility connections (electricity, gas, DTH, broadband).

Pro Tip: Inspect the home with a snag list (checking for leaks, electrical issues, plumbing problems) before moving in.

Key Takeaways

✓ Plan your finances & loan eligibility before searching for properties.

✓ Always verify legal documents to avoid fraud.

✓ Negotiate prices & hidden costs to save lakhs.

✓ Choose the right payment plan & avoid high-interest loans.

✓ Ensure property registration is legally complete before final payment.

What's Next?

In Chapter 13: The Ultimate Real Estate Investment Blueprint, we'll explore how to build a property portfolio, maximize rental income, and create long-term wealth through real estate.

Did You Know?

The Real Estate (Regulation and Development) Act (RERA) transformed India's property market. Within its first year of implementation in 2016, 65% of homebuyers reported faster resolution of complaints against builders in states like Maharashtra and Karnataka.

XIII

The Ultimate Real Estate Investment Blueprint

"The fastest path to financial freedom is owning assets that pay you every month." — Wealth Strategist

13.1 Why Real Estate is the Best Wealth-Building Tool

✓ Cash Flow: Rental income covers EMIs & generates passive income.

✓ Appreciation: Property values increase 8-15% annually in high-growth areas.

✓ Leverage: Buy with 20-30% down payment, while banks fund the rest.

✓ Tax Benefits: Home loans offer   ₹5 lakh+ in tax deductions annually.

Did You Know?

·90% of millionaires worldwide have real estate in their portfolio.

·Smart investors earn   ₹1-5 lakh per month from rental properties.

13.2 The 5-Step Plan to Building a Real Estate Portfolio

✓ Step 1: Start with Your First Investment Property

• Buy a ready-to-move apartment near business hubs (higher rental demand).

• Target rental yield: 3-5% for residential, 6-10% for commercial.

• Use a home loan with tax benefits to reduce costs.

✓ Step 2: Optimize Rental Cash Flow

• Offer fully furnished homes → 20-30% higher rents.

• List on Airbnb & corporate rental platforms for better income.

• Use a property manager to handle tenants (5-10% fee).

✔ Step 3: Leverage Equity to Buy a Second Property

· After 5 years, refinance your first property to buy a second one.

· Use rental income + equity growth to scale investments.

✔ Step 4: Diversify into Commercial & REITs

· Office spaces, retail shops, & warehouses generate higher rental income.

· REITs offer 10-15% annual returns without property maintenance.

✔ Step 5: Exit Strategy & Reinvesting Profits

· Sell properties in 7-10 years to reinvest in high-growth areas.

· 1031 Exchange Strategy (used in the US, coming to India) → Swap one property for another without paying capital gains tax.

Pro Tip: Always reinvest profits into appreciating assets to compound wealth.

13.3 How to Identify High-Return Investment Properties

✔ Look for Areas with High Rental Demand

· Near IT parks, SEZs, metro stations, airports.

· Vacancy rate <5% = High rental demand.

✔ Target 8-12% Annual Appreciation

· Areas with upcoming infrastructure (metro, highways, business hubs).

· Compare 5-year price trends before investing.

Pro Tip: Properties with low maintenance costs + high rental yields are ideal for long-term wealth building.

13.4 The Power of Real Estate Leverage (Using Loans to Grow Faster)

How Smart Investors Use Debt to Multiply Wealth

✔ Buy Property at ₹1 Cr with ₹25L Down Payment

✔ Property Value Grows 10% Yearly → Becomes ₹1.5 Cr in 5 Years

✔ ROI = 100%+ on ₹25L Investment (Using Bank's Money)

Pro Tip: Always keep 6-12 months of EMIs in reserve to avoid financial risk.

13.5 Case Study: How an Investor Built a ₹50 Cr Portfolio in 10 Years

✔ Year 1: Bought ₹50L flat with ₹10L down payment.

✔ Year 3: Refinanced 1st property → Bought 2nd property.

✔ Year 5: Owned 3 properties, earning ₹2L/month in rental income.

✔ Year 10: Built ₹50 Cr portfolio, retired early.

✔ Lesson: Smart leverage + reinvesting profits = Rapid wealth growth.

Key Takeaways

✔ Real estate offers cash flow, appreciation, leverage, and tax benefits.

✔ Build wealth step-by-step: Buy, rent, refinance, reinvest.

✔ Target high-growth locations & properties with strong rental demand.

✔ Use home loans & rental income to scale investments faster.

✔ Plan an exit strategy to maximize profits & minimize tax.

What's Next?

In Chapter 14: Real Estate Market Cycles & Timing Your Investments, we'll explore how to buy low, sell high, and profit from market trends.

Did You Know?

The digital revolution in real estate began modestly—the first online property listing appeared in 1995. Today, Indian PropTech platforms like Housing.com list over a million properties monthly, demonstrating the industry's dramatic digital transformation.

XIV
Real Estate Market Cycles & Timing Your Investments

"Buy when there's blood in the streets, even if the blood is your own." — *Baron Rothschild*

14.1 Why Market Timing is Critical in Real Estate

Real estate, like the stock market, moves in cycles—and knowing when to buy, hold, or sell can mean the difference between a   ₹50 lakh profit or a loss.

✔ *Did You Know?*

·*Investors who bought property in Mumbai in 2009 (after the financial crisis) saw 3x returns by 2018.*

·*Those who bought at 2015 market peak struggled to sell even in 2023 without losses.*

The 4 Phases of the Real Estate Cycle

- Recovery Phase → Low demand, prices stabilizing. (Best for early investors)
- Expansion Phase → Rising demand, high appreciation. (Best for rental income & long-term gains)
- Boom Phase → Peak prices, oversupply risk. (Sell high & take profits!)
- Recession Phase → Prices drop, market corrects. (Best for buying undervalued properties)

Pro Tip: The biggest returns come from buying in recession & selling in boom phases.

14.2 How to Identify the Best Time to Buy Property

✓ Market Indicators for Buying:

? Prices stabilized after a drop (sign of recovery).

? New projects launch at lower prices (builders need buyers).

? Rental yields start increasing (tenant demand rising).

Pro Tip: The best deals happen when banks increase loan rejections & distressed sales rise—it's a sign that the market is at a low point.

14.3 When to Sell: Maximizing Profits at Market Peaks

✓ Market Indicators for Selling:

? Property prices rising faster than rental yields (market overheating).

? Speculative buying increases (too many investors, not enough end-users).

? Government policies increase taxes or loan rates (reduces affordability).

Pro Tip: If your property has appreciated 50-80% in under 5 years, consider selling & reinvesting in an undervalued area.

14.4 Case Study: How an Investor Turned ₹50 Lakh into ₹2 Crore

✓ 2009: Bought an apartment in Gurugram for ₹50L (after 2008 recession).

✓ 2014: Prices soared to ₹1.5 Cr.

✓ 2015: Sold at market peak → Reinvested ₹1.5 Cr into a commercial property.

✓ 2023: Commercial property worth ₹2.2 Cr, generating ₹1.5 lakh/month rental income.

✓ Lesson: Timing the market cycle correctly can multiply your wealth.

14.5 How to Predict the Next Real Estate Boom or Crash

✓ 5 Signs of a Market Boom (Time to Sell)

? Property prices rise 10-15% per year.

? Builders launch too many projects (oversupply risk).

? Speculators buy without intent to live/rent.

? Government policies favor real estate tax hikes.

? Rental yields drop despite rising property prices.

✓ 5 Signs of a Market Crash (Time to Buy)

? Foreclosures & distressed sales increase.

? Developers offer huge discounts & easy payment plans.

? Interest rates rise, reducing buyer demand.

? Rental demand starts rising while prices remain low.

? Banks tighten lending rules, making it harder to get loans.

Pro Tip: Buy when everyone is afraid to invest, sell when everyone is rushing to buy.

Key Takeaways

✓ Real estate cycles follow recovery, expansion, boom, and recession phases.

✓ Smart investors buy during market downturns & sell during peak booms.

✓ Watch for indicators like loan rates, unsold inventory, and rental yields to time your decisions.

✓ Long-term success in real estate comes from timing purchases, not just holding assets indefinitely.

What's Next?

In Chapter 15: Exit Strategies & Tax Planning for Real Estate Investors, we'll cover how to sell property for maximum profit, reduce capital gains tax, and reinvest smartly.

Did You Know?

Mumbai's unique "Pagdi" system, protected under the Rent Control Act of 1947, creates fascinating market dynamics. Some tenants in old buildings pay as little as ₹500/month in rent, while ownership rights often transfer through informal "pagdi" payments worth crores!

XV

Exit Strategies & Tax Planning for Real Estate Investors

"Making money in real estate isn't just about buying right—it's about selling smart." — Wealth Advisor

15.1 Why Exit Strategy is Crucial in Real Estate

Most investors focus on buying property, but few plan when & how to sell for maximum profit. Without a smart exit strategy, you may:

✓ Sell too early and miss out on more appreciation.

✓ Sell too late and lose money in a market downturn.

✓ Pay excessive taxes, losing 20-30% of your profits.

Did You Know?

· Capital gains tax can take away up to 20% of your profits—unless you use legal exemptions.

· Many investors earn millions but lose money due to poor tax planning.

15.2 The Best Time to Sell Your Property for Maximum Profit

✓ Sell When:

? Property value has increased 2X or more from your purchase price.

? Rental yield drops below 2-3%, meaning appreciation has slowed.

? Government policies increase property taxes or loan rates (reducing demand).

? Market is in a boom phase with too many speculative buyers.

✓ Hold or Reinvest If:

? Market is in a downturn or correction phase (selling now = lower profits).

? Rental income is strong and increasing.

? Infrastructure projects (metro, airport, SEZ) are coming up nearby (future appreciation).

Pro Tip: Never sell property just because prices have risen—always compare rental yields vs. reinvestment opportunities.

15.3 Capital Gains Tax & How to Reduce It

Types of Capital Gains Tax (CGT) in India

Type

Holding Period

Tax Rate

Short-Term Capital Gains (STCG)

Sold within 2 years

Taxed as per income slab (10-30%)

Long-Term Capital Gains (LTCG)

Sold after 2 years

20% with indexation benefits

Pro Tip: Always hold real estate for at least 2 years to avoid higher short-term taxes.

15.4 Tax Exemptions & Loopholes to Save Lakhs

1. Section 54: Reinvest in Another Property (Best for Homeowners & Investors)

✓ Sell an old property → Buy a new one within 2 years → No LTCG tax.

✓ New property must be in India, residential, and held for at least 3 years.

Example:

• Sold a   ₹2 crore house → Made   ₹80 lakh profit.

• Bought a new house for   ₹1.5 crore → Paid   ₹0 tax under Section 54.

2. Section 54EC: Invest in Capital Gains Bonds (Best for Investors Looking for Tax-Free Returns)

✓ Sell property → Invest profit (up to   ₹50 lakh) in NHAI/REC bonds within 6 months → Zero LTCG tax.

✓ Bonds have a 5-year lock-in with 5.25% annual interest.

Example:

• Sold a shop for   ₹1 crore →   ₹40 lakh capital gain.

• Invested in NHAI bonds → Saved   ₹8 lakh in tax.

3. 1031 Exchange (Coming to India) (Best for Property Flippers & Investors)

✓ Swap one property for another without paying tax on capital gains.

✓ Used in the US real estate market, expected to be introduced in India soon.

Pro Tip: If reinvesting in property, ensure all sale proceeds go directly into the new purchase to qualify for tax exemptions.

15.5 Best Exit Strategies for Different Investors

✓ For Homeowners:

? Sell only if upgrading to a better home or relocating.

? Use Section 54 exemption to avoid LTCG tax.

✓ For Investors:

? Sell when rental yield drops below 2-3%.

? Reinvest in high-growth Tier-2 cities for better returns.

✓ For NRIs:

? Tax deducted at source (TDS) = 20% on LTCG → File for a refund if exemptions apply.

? Consider REITs for lower tax liability.

Pro Tip: Selling property near a metro launch or IT hub expansion can increase your sale price by 20-30% more.

15.6 Case Study: How an Investor Saved ₹25 Lakh in Taxes

✓ Sold a ₹1.5 crore apartment in Mumbai after 5 years.

✓ Profit = ₹60 lakh (LTCG tax = ₹12 lakh).

✓ Reinvested ₹55 lakh in another property under Section 54.

✓ Final tax paid = ₹0.

Lesson: Smart tax planning can turn a ₹12 lakh tax bill into ₹0.

Key Takeaways

✓ Sell when prices peak, rental yields drop, or demand slows.

✓ Hold for 2+ years to qualify for lower long-term capital gains tax.

✓ Use Section 54 (reinvestment) or Section 54EC (capital gains bonds) to reduce tax.

✓ Plan your next investment before selling to optimize profits.

✓ Avoid selling in downturns—rent instead & wait for market recovery.

What's Next?

In Chapter 16: The Psychology of Real Estate Investing, we'll explore how emotions impact buying decisions, behavioral biases, and how smart investors avoid psychological traps.

Did You Know?

The world's most expensive private residence, Antilia in Mumbai, owned by Mukesh Ambani, is valued at ₹15,000 crore ($2 billion). This 27-floor vertical mansion features three helipads and requires a staff of 600 to maintain, with monthly electricity bills reaching ₹70 lakh!

XVI

The Psychology of Real Estate Investing

"Emotions drive real estate decisions, but data builds wealth." — *Investment Psychologist*

16.1 Why Psychology Matters in Real Estate Investing

Real estate is not just about numbers—it's about psychology. Buyers and investors often:

✓ Overpay due to fear of missing out (FOMO).

✓ Hold onto bad investments too long, hoping for a turnaround.

✓ Make emotional decisions instead of using data.

Did You Know?

·80% of real estate buyers make emotional decisions rather than data-driven ones.

·Fear, greed, and social pressure cause most investment mistakes.

16.2 Common Psychological Traps in Real Estate

1. The "Forever Home" Fallacy (Homebuyers' Mistake)

✓ Many buyers believe their first home must be perfect forever.

✓ Reality: Most people move within 7-10 years due to job changes, family needs, or better investment opportunities.

Pro Tip: Buy a starter home that fits your current needs without overextending your budget.

2. The Fear of Missing Out (FOMO) Trap (Investor's Mistake)

✓ Buyers rush into overpriced markets fearing "Prices will never drop."

✓ Reality: Markets always move in cycles—what rises fast can also crash.

Example: Many buyers rushed to buy in 2014's overpriced market and saw flat or negative returns for years.

Pro Tip: If everyone is rushing to buy, step back and analyze if fundamentals justify the price rise.

3. The Endowment Effect (Overvaluing Your Own Property)

✔ Homeowners overestimate their property's value due to emotional attachment.

✔ Reality: Buyers care about market rates, not your memories.

Pro Tip: Price your property based on recent sales, not your personal expectations.

4. The Loss Aversion Trap (Holding a Bad Investment Too Long)

✔ Investors refuse to sell at a loss, hoping for recovery.

✔ Reality: A bad property rarely becomes a great investment.

Pro Tip: Cut losses if rental yield is below 2-3% and appreciation is stagnant.

16.3 The Science of Smart Real Estate Decisions

1. Use Data, Not Emotions

✔ Track price trends, rental yields, infrastructure growth before buying.

✔ Ignore hype & media panic—trust market fundamentals.

Example: Investors who bought in Bengaluru's Whitefield in 2005 (based on IT expansion data) saw 5X appreciation by 2020.

2. Compare Rent vs. Buy Ratios

✔ If renting is 3X cheaper than buying, rent & invest elsewhere.

✔ Use the Price-to-Rent Ratio Formula:

Benchmark:

· Below 15 → Buying is better.

· Above 20 → Renting is smarter.

3. Avoid Social Proof Investing (Buying Just Because Others Are Buying)

✔ Many buyers purchase in hyped areas without checking fundamentals.

✔ Smart investors buy in undervalued markets before the hype.

Pro Tip: Buy in areas with low prices but strong future infrastructure plans (metro, IT parks, highways).

16.4 How to Think Like a Professional Investor

✔ Patience is Key → Real estate cycles take 5-10 years to generate returns.

✔ Cash Flow First → Focus on rental yield & affordability before speculation.

✓ Numbers Over Emotions → If a property doesn't meet ROI targets, don't buy it.

✓ Pro Tip: Think like a landlord, not just a homeowner. Buy properties that make financial sense, not just emotional sense.

16.5 Case Study: How an Investor Avoided a ₹50 Lakh Mistake

✓ 2017: Investor considered buying a ₹2 Cr luxury apartment in Mumbai.

✓ FOMO pressured him to book fast, but he waited.

✓ 2019 Market Crash: The same flat was available for ₹1.5 Cr (₹50 lakh cheaper).

Lesson: Smart investors wait for market cycles instead of rushing into purchases.

Key Takeaways

✓ Real estate is an emotional decision—but investing should be data-driven.

✓ Avoid FOMO, social proof investing, and overpaying due to hype.

✓ Always compare rent vs. buy ratios before purchasing.

✓ Think like an investor—focus on cash flow & long-term growth.

What's Next?

In Chapter 17: The Future of Real Estate Careers & Entrepreneurship, we'll explore high-growth job opportunities, real estate startups, and how to build a career in this booming industry.

Did You Know?

Success in real estate can come from unexpected places. Housing.com, founded by 12 college dropouts in 2012, was sold for ₹1,800 crore in 2020. This success story proves that innovation and determination can lead to extraordinary achievements in the real estate sector.

XVII

The Future of Real Estate Careers & Entrepreneurship

"Real estate is not just about properties—it's about building businesses, creating wealth, and shaping cities." — Industry Leader

17.1 Why Real Estate is One of India's Fastest-Growing Careers

The real estate sector is projected to grow to $1 trillion by 2030, making it one of India's largest employment generators.

✔ Over 75 million people work in Indian real estate.

✔ The demand for brokers, property managers, PropTech founders, and commercial developers is increasing.

✔ Foreign investments & new infrastructure projects will drive growth for the next two decades.

Did You Know?

• India needs 25 million new homes by 2030, ensuring continuous job opportunities.

• The rise of PropTech startups (AI, blockchain, digital property platforms) is creating high-paying tech jobs in real estate.

17.2 Top Career Paths in Real Estate & Their Earnings

1. Real Estate Broker (Residential & Commercial Sales)

✔ Helps buyers and sellers close deals.

✔ Commissions: 1-2% of transaction value (can earn ₹50L+ annually).

✔ Works independently or with a real estate firm.

Pro Tip: Specializing in luxury real estate or commercial sales increases commissions significantly.

2. Property Consultant & Investment Advisor

✓ Advises clients on profitable real estate investments.

✓ Works with NRIs, HNIs (high-net-worth individuals), and corporate investors.

✓ Earnings: ₹10L - ₹1 Cr+ annually (commission-based).

Pro Tip: Learn RERA laws & taxation to stand out as a top consultant.

3. Real Estate Developer & Builder

✓ Develops residential & commercial projects.

✓ Requires land acquisition, funding, and project execution skills.

✓ Profit margins: 20-50% per project.

Pro Tip: Start small—JV partnerships with landowners reduce capital requirements.

4. PropTech & Real Estate Startup Founder

✓ Builds technology-driven real estate platforms (renting, buying, home services).

✓ Examples: NoBroker, 99acres, MagicBricks, Housing.com.

✓ Startup funding potential: $100M+ raised by PropTech companies in India.

Pro Tip: AI-driven platforms for property price predictions & digital transactions are the future.

5. Real Estate Lawyer (Property Law & Litigation)

✓ Specializes in land disputes, property agreements, RERA compliance.

✓ Works with developers, investors, and buyers.

✓ Earnings: ₹8L - ₹50L per year.

Pro Tip: Master RERA laws & land acquisition rules to become an in-demand legal expert.

6. Real Estate Influencer & Digital Marketer

✓ Uses YouTube, Instagram, LinkedIn to promote real estate projects & advisory services.

✓ Monetizes via sponsorships, affiliate marketing, and consulting.

✓ Earnings: ₹5L - ₹30L per year (depends on audience size).

Pro Tip: Drone property tours & market insights videos attract high-end buyers & investors.

17.3 Starting a Real Estate Brokerage or Investment Firm

✓ Step 1: Get an RERA Broker License (Mandatory for real estate agents).

✓ Step 2: Specialize in luxury homes, commercial properties, or investment advisory.

✓ Step 3: Use AI-driven lead generation & digital marketing to attract high-value clients.

✓ Step 4: Build relationships with developers & financial institutions for exclusive deals.

Pro Tip: Exclusive property deals & personalized service help brokers charge higher commissions.

17.4 Future Trends in Real Estate Careers

✓ AI & Virtual Property Tours → 3D home tours & AI-powered home matching.

✓ Co-Living & Shared Spaces Management → High rental demand in metro cities.

✓ Green Building Consultants → Focus on sustainability & energy efficiency.

✓ Fractional Ownership & REIT Advisors → Helping investors buy shares in real estate.

Pro Tip: Tech-driven, customer-focused real estate services will dominate the future.

17.5 Case Study: How a Broker Built a ₹10 Crore Business in 5 Years

✓ 2018: Started as an independent real estate agent in Bengaluru.

✓ 2019: Focused on luxury real estate & NRI investors.

✓ 2021: Expanded into commercial property leasing.

✓ 2023: Built a ₹10 Cr+ turnover firm with a team of 20+ agents.

Lesson: Niche specialization & digital marketing are key to success.

Key Takeaways

✓ Real estate careers offer unlimited earnings in sales, investment consulting, PropTech, and development.

✓ Brokers & investment advisors can earn ₹10L - ₹1 Cr+ annually through commissions.

✓ PropTech startups are the next big opportunity in real estate.

✓ Future careers will be driven by AI, digital transactions, and sustainable development.

What's Next?

In Chapter 18: Real Estate in the Global Economy, we'll explore how global markets impact Indian real estate, foreign investment trends, and international buying opportunities.

Did You Know?

House hunters typically make their decision within the first 7-10 seconds of entering a property. The entryway's impact is so crucial that real estate experts call this the "rule of 10" – suggesting that prospective buyers form 80% of their overall opinion about a house in just those first moments.

XVIII

Real Estate in the Global Economy

"Real estate is no longer a local business—it's a global wealth-building tool." — International Investment Consultant

18.1 How Global Trends Impact Indian Real Estate

The Indian real estate market is deeply connected to global economic trends, including:

✓ Foreign Direct Investment (FDI) inflows into Indian infrastructure.

✓ Interest rate policies of the US Federal Reserve & global central banks.

✓ Global recessions & economic slowdowns affecting investor sentiment.

✓ Trends in remote work & global mobility changing housing demand.

Did You Know?

· *In 2022, NRIs invested $13.3 billion in Indian real estate, up 12% from 2021.*

· *100% FDI is allowed in India's real estate sector, boosting large-scale investments.*

18.2 The Rise of Foreign Investment in Indian Real Estate

1. Why Foreign Investors Are Choosing India

✓ High rental yields & lower property prices compared to developed markets.

✓ Growing commercial real estate sector (office spaces, warehouses).

✓ Government policies (REITs, FDI, RERA) increasing transparency.

✓ Top Foreign Investors in Indian Real Estate

? Blackstone Group (US) – Invested $6 billion in Indian commercial properties.

? Brookfield Asset Management (Canada) – Owns major office parks in India.

? GIC (Singapore) – Invested in rental housing & logistics hubs.

Pro Tip: Foreign investment strengthens Tier-1 & Tier-2 city real estate markets by increasing demand.

18.3 How Global Economic Shifts Affect Indian Real Estate

✓ US Interest Rate Hikes → Reduce foreign investments in Indian property.

✓ Global Recessions (Like 2008, 2020 Pandemic) → Delay new real estate projects.

✓ China's Slowdown → Pushes global investors to shift capital to India.

Pro Tip: Real estate prices rise during global economic booms & slow during crises—buy low, sell high.

18.4 Best Countries for Indians to Buy Property Abroad

Many Indians are investing in foreign real estate for:

✓ Higher rental income.

✓ Visa & residency benefits.

✓ Diversification of assets.

Top Destinations for Indian Property Investors

Country

Why Invest?

Dubai (UAE)

Tax-free income, easy investor visas, high rental yields (6-8%)

London (UK)

Safe investment, strong appreciation, access to EU markets

Singapore

Stable economy, high demand for rental properties

Canada

Residency through real estate investment, growing housing market

US (New York, Texas, Florida)

High appreciation & rental demand in major cities

Pro Tip: Dubai offers Golden Visa options for investors buying minimum ₹ 4 Cr+ properties.

18.5 Buying Property Abroad: What Indian Investors Should Know

✓ Legal & Tax Rules

? Some countries limit foreign ownership (Thailand, Switzerland).

? Indian RBI rules allow $250,000 per year per person for foreign investments.

✔ Financing Options

? Many banks don't offer home loans for overseas property purchases—cash buyers have an advantage.

✔ Taxation

? Rental income from foreign properties is taxable in India, but double taxation treaties reduce liabilities.

Pro Tip: Set up an NRI account for seamless overseas property transactions.

18.6 Case Study: How an Indian Investor Earned 12% Returns in Dubai

✔ 2019: Investor bought a ₹3 Cr luxury apartment in Dubai Marina.

✔ Rented it out for ₹1.8 lakh/month (7.2% rental yield).

✔ 2023: Property appreciated by ₹1.2 Cr.

✔ Total Returns: 12% per year (rental + appreciation).

Lesson: Dubai's tax-free rental income & Golden Visa incentives make it a top choice for Indian investors.

Key Takeaways

✔ India's real estate market is growing due to foreign investments & global demand.

✔ NRIs & global funds are increasing investments in Indian properties.

✔ Economic trends (interest rates, recessions) impact real estate cycles.

✔ Dubai, UK, US, and Canada are top global destinations for Indian investors.

✔ Always check legal, tax, and financing options before buying property abroad.

What's Next?

In Chapter 19: Real Estate Technology & The PropTech Revolution, we'll explore how AI, blockchain, smart contracts, and digital platforms are transforming the real estate industry.

Did You Know?

Ancient Roman apartments called "insulae" were the world's first high-rise residential buildings, often reaching 7-8 stories tall. These apartments even featured sophisticated amenities like running water and heating systems, though only ground floor units were typically reserved for wealthy tenants due to the risk of collapse and fires in upper floors.

XIX

Real Estate Technology & The PropTech Revolution

"The future of real estate isn't just about properties—it's about technology reshaping how we buy, sell, and invest." — PropTech Founder

19.1 How Technology is Disrupting Real Estate

The real estate industry is shifting from traditional, offline transactions to digital, AI-driven, and blockchain-secured processes.

✓ AI is predicting property prices & rental trends.

✓ Blockchain is eliminating fraud & making transactions secure.

✓ PropTech startups are reducing brokerage fees & improving efficiency.

Did You Know?

· PropTech investment in India exceeded $1.5 billion in 2023.

· 80% of property searches in India now start online.

· AI & blockchain are expected to cut real estate fraud by 50% in the next decade.

19.2 AI & Big Data: The Future of Real Estate Decisions

✓ AI-Powered Property Valuation

· AI predicts future price appreciation based on historical trends, infrastructure projects & demand-supply ratios.

· Example: AI-driven platforms like Square Yards & NoBroker help buyers analyze price trends.

✓ AI Matching Buyers & Sellers

• Smart algorithms match buyers with properties based on lifestyle, commute time, and affordability.

✓ Predictive Analytics for Investment Decisions

• AI identifies emerging real estate hotspots before they boom.

• Example: Bengaluru's Whitefield saw AI-driven demand forecasting in early 2010s, leading to massive appreciation.

Pro Tip: Use AI-powered real estate tools to assess price trends before buying or investing.

19.3 Blockchain & Smart Contracts: The End of Real Estate Fraud?

✓ Blockchain-Based Land Registries

• Eliminates land record fraud by storing ownership history on a tamper-proof ledger.

• Example: Telangana launched India's first blockchain land registry in 2022.

✓ Smart Contracts: Instant Property Transfers

• Digitally executed agreements that eliminate the need for middlemen.

• Speeds up title transfers, lease agreements, and rental payments.

✓ Fractional Property Ownership Using Blockchain

• Allows small investors to own a share of a high-value property via tokenization.

• Example: A ₹50 Cr commercial building can be split into ₹1 lakh digital shares.

Pro Tip: Watch for Indian REITs launching tokenized real estate investments in the next 5 years.

19.4 Virtual Reality (VR) & Augmented Reality (AR) in Real Estate

✓ VR Property Tours

• Buyers can walk through homes digitally without visiting in person.

• Example: 3D home tours on MagicBricks & Housing.com are now standard.

✓ Augmented Reality (AR) Interior Planning

• Overlay furniture & renovation ideas before buying.

• Example: IKEA's AR home design app lets users visualize furniture in real space.

Pro Tip: Expect 90% of property searches to be VR-enabled by 2030.

19.5 PropTech Startups Transforming Indian Real Estate

Startup

What It Does

NoBroker

Eliminates brokers, reducing buying & renting costs.

MagicBricks

AI-powered property recommendations.

Square Yards

Digital mortgage & AI-driven investment insights.

Strata

Fractional ownership of commercial properties.

PropertyShare

Blockchain-based REIT investments.

Pro Tip: Invest early in PropTech startups or use their platforms for cost savings.

19.6 The Future of Smart Cities & IoT in Real Estate

✓ IoT-Enabled Smart Homes

· Smart thermostats, voice-controlled lighting, and AI security systems are becoming standard.

· Example: Mumbai's Lodha Palava City integrates AI-driven smart home features.

✓ 5G & Real Estate Transactions

· Faster internet = Seamless digital transactions & instant legal verifications.

✓ Smart Cities Using AI for Urban Planning

· AI optimizes traffic, pollution control, and green spaces.

· Example: Dholera Smart City, Gujarat, is India's first AI-driven urban development project.

Pro Tip: Investing in smart city projects guarantees high appreciation in the next decade.

19.7 Case Study: How an Investor Used PropTech to Earn ₹20L Extra

✓ 2018: Investor used AI valuation tools to identify undervalued properties in Hyderabad.

✓ 2019: Bought a 3BHK for ₹60L based on predictive price appreciation data.

✓ 2023: Sold it for ₹1.2 Cr after metro expansion, doubling returns in 5 years.

Lesson: AI-driven real estate analytics help investors make better decisions.

Key Takeaways

✓ AI, blockchain, and VR are transforming real estate transactions & investments.

✓ Smart contracts & tokenized ownership will reduce fraud & increase accessibility.

✓ PropTech startups are lowering costs & increasing efficiency in buying, selling & renting.

✓ Smart city investments will be the next big real estate boom.

What's Next?

In Chapter 20: Conclusion & The Road Ahead, we'll summarize key learnings, future trends, and a final roadmap for homebuyers & investors.

Did You Know?

There's a curious economic theory called the "Skyscraper Index" which suggests that the construction of the world's tallest buildings often coincides with economic crises. The Empire State Building (1931), World Trade Center (1973), and Burj Khalifa (2010) were all completed during or just before major economic downturns.

XX
Conclusion & The Road Ahead

"The best investment on Earth is Earth itself." — Louis Glickman

20.1 The Real Estate Journey: From Beginner to Expert

This book has covered every essential aspect of real estate, from home buying & legal safeguards to investment strategies & PropTech innovations. Whether you're a first-time homebuyer, a real estate investor, or an aspiring entrepreneur, these insights will help you navigate the industry with confidence.

20.2 The Most Important Lessons From This Book

✓ Homebuyers must always verify legal documents, builder reputation & RERA registration.

✓ Real estate investing is about location, rental yield, market cycles & strategic exits.

✓ Negotiation & financing strategies can save lakhs in costs & interest payments.

✓ Government policies (RERA, REITs, FDI) have transformed the industry, ensuring more transparency.

✓ PropTech, AI & blockchain will dominate the future of real estate transactions.

Pro Tip: The best real estate investors think long-term, buy undervalued properties, and reinvest profits wisely.

20.3 The Future of Indian Real Estate (2025-2040)

✔ Urbanization Will Accelerate → India will need 25M+ new homes by 2030.

✔ Tier-2 & Tier-3 Cities Will Boom → Infrastructure projects will drive 50% of future real estate growth.

✔ Sustainable & Smart Homes Will Become the Standard → AI-driven smart homes & energy-efficient buildings will dominate demand.

✔ Real Estate Will Become More Digital → AI, blockchain & PropTech startups will replace traditional brokers & paperwork-heavy transactions.

Pro Tip: Investing in emerging cities & AI-driven smart communities will yield maximum appreciation.

20.4 A Final Roadmap for Homebuyers & Investors

For First-Time Homebuyers:

? Set a budget, check loan eligibility, & compare locations.

? Always verify legal documents, RERA registration & approvals.

? Negotiate price & hidden costs before signing any agreement.

For Real Estate Investors:

? Buy undervalued properties in high-growth zones.

? Focus on rental income & cash flow before appreciation.

? Exit smartly—sell when prices peak, reinvest in new markets.

For Entrepreneurs & Real Estate Professionals:

? Specialize in luxury, commercial, or PropTech-driven real estate services.

? Use AI & blockchain tools to enhance efficiency & transparency.

? Build long-term client relationships for sustained business growth.

Pro Tip: The key to success in real estate is strategy, patience, and adaptability.

20.5 Final Words: The Best Time to Start is Now

Whether you're buying your first home, expanding your investment portfolio, or starting a real estate business, the best time to act is now.

✔ Real estate rewards long-term thinkers.

✔ Opportunities exist in every market cycle—if you know where to look.

✔ With the right knowledge & strategy, real estate can secure your financial future.

Pro Tip: Always stay informed, network with industry experts, and keep an eye on future trends.

The Road Ahead: What You Should Do Next

? Homebuyers: Start by shortlisting RERA-approved properties in high-demand locations.

? Investors: Research rental yield, cash flow & future infrastructure developments before buying.

? Entrepreneurs: Leverage AI, blockchain & PropTech tools to create innovative real estate solutions.

Final Thought: Real estate success isn't about luck—it's about knowledge, timing & execution.

The End

Glossary Of Real Estate Terms

This glossary provides definitions of key real estate terms used throughout the book. Understanding these terms will help homebuyers, investors, and real estate professionals make informed decisions.

A

Affordable Housing: Housing projects that are priced lower to cater to middle- and lower-income groups, often supported by government schemes.

Appreciation: The increase in a property's value over time due to demand, infrastructure development, or inflation.

B

Balance Transfer: Moving an existing home loan to another bank to benefit from lower interest rates.

Brokerage Fee: The commission paid to real estate agents or brokers for facilitating a property deal.

C

Capital Gains Tax (CGT): The tax levied on profits made from selling property, classified as Short-Term or Long-Term Capital Gains (LTCG).

Carpet Area: The actual usable floor space inside a property, excluding walls and common areas.

D

Down Payment: The initial amount paid by the buyer while taking a home loan, usually 15-30% of the property value.

Due Diligence: Legal and financial verification of a property before purchase.

E

Encumbrance Certificate (EC): A document proving that a property has no legal or financial liabilities (like unpaid loans).

Equated Monthly Installment (EMI): The fixed monthly payment made to repay a home loan.

F

Fair Market Value: The estimated price a property would sell for in the open market.

Floor Rise Charges: Extra charges levied by builders for properties on higher floors.

G

Green Building: A property designed with eco-friendly features like solar panels, rainwater harvesting, and energy-efficient materials.

I

Inflation-Linked Rent Increase: A clause in rental agreements that increases rent annually based on inflation rates.

Infrastructure Impact on Real Estate: The effect of roads, metro stations, and business parks on property values.

L

Lease Agreement: A legally binding contract between a landlord and tenant outlining rental terms.

Loan-to-Value Ratio (LTV): The percentage of a property's value that can be borrowed as a loan.

M

Market Value: The price a property can fetch under normal conditions.

Mutation Certificate: A document issued by local authorities confirming property ownership transfer.

N

NRI Investment Rules: Regulations governing real estate investments by Non-Resident Indians (NRIs).

No Objection Certificate (NOC): A legal document stating that there are no objections to property construction or sale.

O

Occupancy Certificate (OC): A document confirming that a building is legally fit for occupancy.

Off-Plan Property: A property that is sold before construction is completed.

R

Real Estate Investment Trust (REIT): A financial instrument allowing small investors to invest in commercial real estate.

Ready-to-Move Property: A fully constructed property available for immediate possession.

RERA (Real Estate Regulatory Authority): The governing body that ensures transparency in real estate transactions.

S

Stamp Duty: A government tax paid to register a property under the buyer's name.

Super Built-Up Area: The total built-up area including common spaces like lobbies and lifts.

T

Title Deed: A legal document proving ownership of a property.

Token Money: A small advance paid to confirm a property booking before finalizing the deal.

This section includes sources, reports, and market research that informed the insights in this book.

Government Reports & Policies

✓ The Real Estate (Regulation and Development) Act, 2016 (RERA) – Government of India

✓ Pradhan Mantri Awas Yojana (PMAY) Guidelines – Ministry of Housing and Urban Affairs

✓ India's Housing Market Outlook 2025 – Reserve Bank of India

Market Research Reports

✓ Knight Frank India: India Real Estate Report (2023)

✓ JLL India: Emerging Investment Trends in Indian Real Estate

✓ Colliers India: Real Estate Market Cycles and Forecasts

Online Real Estate Portals & Data Sources

✓ MagicBricks.com – Market trends, rental yields, home loan comparisons

✓ 99Acres.com – Housing trends, new project launches, and builder ratings

✓ Housing.com – AI-driven property price predictions and buyer insights

PropTech & Emerging Trends

✓ Blockchain in Real Estate: Smart Contracts & Digital Transactions – Harvard Business Review

✓ The Impact of AI & Big Data in Real Estate Pricing – McKinsey & Company

Books on Real Estate & Investment

✓ "The Millionaire Real Estate Investor" – Gary Keller

✓ "Rich Dad, Poor Dad" – Robert Kiyosaki (For understanding wealth-building through real estate)

✓ "Mastering the Art of Commercial Real Estate Investing" – Doug Marshall

Pro Tip: Always refer to official RERA portals, RBI home loan policies, and global real estate reports for up-to-date market insights.

INDIA'S REAL ESTATE TYCOONS – THE VISIONARIES SHAPING THE INDUSTRY

"Behind every iconic city skyline, there are visionaries who dared to dream bigger." — *Industry Expert*

The Builders of Modern India

India's real estate landscape has been transformed by a handful of visionary developers and entrepreneurs who have built entire cities, pioneered sustainable living, and expanded India's global real estate footprint. These business leaders have not only amassed immense wealth but have also reshaped urban living, commercial real estate, and infrastructure development.

This chapter explores the top real estate tycoons of India, their achievements, and the impact they have had on the industry.

India's Top 10 Richest Real Estate Personalities (As of 2023, based on Forbes, Hurun India, and industry reports)

1. Mangal Prabhat Lodha – The Luxury Housing King

✓ Net Worth: $15.1 billion

✓ Company: Lodha Group (Macrotech Developers)

✓ Major Projects: World Towers (Mumbai), Trump Tower Mumbai, Palava City, 10 Grosvenor Square (London)

✓ Achievements:

• India's richest real estate tycoon, Lodha built Mumbai's tallest residential tower and expanded into London's high-end property market.

• His Palava City is India's largest privately planned smart city.

2. Rajiv Singh – The Cyber City Developer

✓ Net Worth: $14.2 billion

✓ Company: DLF Ltd.

✓ Major Projects: DLF Cyber City (Gurgaon), DLF Downtown, DLF Emporio (Luxury Mall), DLF Golf Course

✓ Achievements:

• Under his leadership, DLF has become India's largest real estate developer, specializing in commercial hubs.

• DLF Cyber City houses major corporations like Google, Microsoft, and Accenture.

3. Vikram Oberoi – Mumbai's Luxury Real Estate Leader

✓ Net Worth: $4.7 billion

✓ Company: Oberoi Realty

✓ Major Projects: Oberoi Sky City, Oberoi Mall, Trump Tower Mumbai
✓ Achievements:
· Specializes in luxury apartments and high-end commercial properties.
· Developing India's tallest residential tower in Oberoi Sky City.

4. Jitendra Virwani – The REIT King

✓ Net Worth: $3.9 billion
✓ Company: Embassy Group
✓ Major Projects: Embassy Manyata Business Park, Embassy TechVillage, Embassy Office Parks REIT
✓ Achievements:
· Created India's first & largest REIT (Real Estate Investment Trust).
· Embassy REIT owns 44 million sq. ft. of commercial real estate, leased to top global companies.

5. Niranjan Hiranandani – The Township Visionary

✓ Net Worth: $3.5 billion
✓ Company: Hiranandani Group
✓ Major Projects: Hiranandani Gardens (Powai), Hiranandani Fortune City (Panvel), Yotta Data Centers
✓ Achievements:
· Developed self-sufficient townships, transforming areas like Powai & Thane into premium residential hubs.
· Diversified into data centers & co-living spaces.

6. Chandru Raheja – The Retail & Hospitality Giant

✓ Net Worth: $3.2 billion
✓ Company: K Raheja Corp
✓ Major Projects: Inorbit Malls, Mindspace IT Parks, Taj Santacruz Hotel, Raheja Exotica
✓ Achievements:
· Pioneered India's modern shopping malls and luxury hotel developments.
· Developed IT parks for global tech firms in Mumbai, Pune, and Hyderabad.

7. Rakesh Wadhawan & Sarang Wadhawan – The Slum Redevelopers

✓ Net Worth: $2.8 billion
✓ Company: HDIL (Housing Development and Infrastructure Ltd.)
✓ Major Projects: Dharavi Redevelopment, Virar Sky City, HDIL Towers
✓ Achievements:

• Specialized in slum rehabilitation projects, notably redeveloping Mumbai's Dharavi slum.

• Faced legal troubles but retained control over major real estate assets.

8. PNC Menon – The Quality Builder

✓ Net Worth: $2.5 billion

✓ Company: Sobha Ltd.

✓ Major Projects: Sobha City, Sobha Dream Acres, Sobha Hartland (Dubai)

✓ Achievements:

• Introduced vertical integration in real estate, controlling every step of construction.

• Expanded into Middle Eastern markets, bringing Indian real estate expertise to Dubai & Oman.

9. Irfan Razack – The Prestige Developer

✓ Net Worth: $2.3 billion

✓ Company: Prestige Group

✓ Major Projects: Prestige Shantiniketan, Prestige Falcon City, Prestige City (Mumbai)

✓ Achievements:

• Bengaluru's leading real estate developer, now expanding into Mumbai & Hyderabad.

• Known for integrated luxury townships and commercial spaces.

10. Kushal Pal Singh – The Father of Gurgaon's Growth

✓ Net Worth: $2.1 billion

✓ Company: DLF Ltd. (Emeritus Chairman)

✓ Major Projects: DLF CyberHub, DLF Phase 1-5, DLF Promenade Mall

✓ Achievements:

• Transformed Gurgaon from rural land into India's corporate capital.

• Retired but remains an industry legend for shaping India's modern real estate industry.

Key Trends Shaping India's Real Estate Future

1. The Rise of Luxury Housing

✓ High demand for ultra-premium apartments in Mumbai, Delhi, and Bengaluru.

✓ Developers like Lodha, Oberoi, and Prestige focus on high-end homes for HNIs & NRIs.

2. Commercial Real Estate & REITs Boom

✔ DLF, Embassy, and Raheja dominate Grade-A office space, attracting global firms.

✔ REITs are becoming a mainstream investment option for retail investors.

3. Smart Cities & Townships Expansion

✔ Hiranandani, Lodha, and Prestige are developing large-scale townships with sustainable infrastructure.

✔ Government projects like Dholera Smart City will create new investment opportunities.

4. Data Centers & PropTech Growth

✔ Developers like Hiranandani & Embassy are investing in data centers & AI-driven real estate.

✔ PropTech platforms like NoBroker & Housing.com are changing how properties are bought & sold.

Lessons from India's Real Estate Tycoons

✔ Think Long-Term: Most real estate billionaires built their wealth over decades by holding assets.

✔ Invest in Commercial & Rental Income: The biggest fortunes come from commercial leases & rental portfolios.

✔ Follow Infrastructure Growth: Smart investors buy before infrastructure projects like metro lines & highways are completed.

✔ Embrace Technology: Future real estate leaders integrate AI, blockchain, and green building solutions.

The 10 Richest Real Estate Personalities In The World (2023)

Data compiled from Forbes, Bloomberg, and the Hurun Global Rich List.

1. Lee Shau Kee (Hong Kong) – The Visionary Builder

✓ Net Worth: $30 billion

✓ Company: Henderson Land Development

✓ Key Assets: International Finance Centre (IFC), The Harbourside

✓ Legacy: Hong Kong's property boom leader, built skyscrapers that define the skyline.

2. Donald Bren (USA) – The California King

✓ Net Worth: $17 billion

✓ Company: Irvine Company

✓ Key Assets: Newport Center, Fashion Island Mall

✓ Legacy: Master-planned 110M+ sq. ft. of real estate in California.

3. Wang Jianlin (China) – Asia's Real Estate Mogul

✓ Net Worth: $15 billion

✓ Company: Dalian Wanda Group

✓ Key Assets: Wanda Plazas, Waldorf Astoria Beijing

✓ Legacy: Once China's richest man, shifted from real estate to entertainment.

4. Stephen Ross (USA) – The Hudson Yards Developer

✓ Net Worth: $12.5 billion

✓ Company: Related Companies

✓ Key Assets: Hudson Yards, Miami Dolphins (NFL)

✓ Legacy: Built NYC's most expensive megaproject.

5. Kwok Family (Hong Kong) – The ICC Tower Builders

✓ Net Worth: $11.8 billion

✓ Company: Sun Hung Kai Properties

✓ Key Assets: ICC Tower, Harbour City Mall

✓ Legacy: Hong Kong's largest developer with 2.4M+ sq. ft. of retail space.

6. Gerald Cavendish Grosvenor & Family (UK) – The Duke of Mayfair

✓ Net Worth: $11 billion

✓ Company: Grosvenor Group

✓ Key Assets: Mayfair, Belgravia (London), Park Royal (Vancouver)

✓ Legacy: Owns some of the most expensive land in London.

7. Harry Triguboff (Australia) – The Apartment Tycoon

✓ Net Worth: $10.5 billion

✓ Company: Meriton

✓ Key Assets: 77,000+ apartments in Sydney & Brisbane

✓ Legacy: Australia's largest high-rise apartment developer.

8. Joseph Lau (Hong Kong) – The Collector Investor

✓ Net Worth: $10 billion

✓ Company: Chinese Estates Holdings

✓ Key Assets: The Zenith, The One Mall

✓ Legacy: Real estate and luxury art investments.

9. Zhang Li (China) – Guangzhou's Real Estate Baron

✓ Net Worth: $9.5 billion

✓ Company: Guangzhou R&F Properties

✓ Key Assets: R&F Centre, Ritz-Carlton hotels

✓ Legacy: Built 50M+ sq. ft. of commercial & residential projects.

10. Sam Zell (USA) – The Real Estate Turnaround Expert

✓ Net Worth: $6.2 billion

✓ Company: Equity Group Investments

✓ Key Assets: Logistics parks, REITs

✓ Legacy: Sold Equity Office Properties for $39 billion in 2007.

Key Trends Shaping Global Real Estate Wealth

✓ 1. Asia Leads in Real Estate Billionaires

• 12 of the 25 richest developers are from China, Hong Kong, or Singapore.

• Urbanization and luxury housing demand fuel market growth.

✓ 2. The Rise of Megaprojects

• Hudson Yards (NYC), Victoria Dockside (Hong Kong), and Dubai's Festival City set new real estate investment benchmarks.

• These multi-billion-dollar mixed-use projects combine offices, luxury homes, retail, and entertainment.

✓ 3. Institutional Investors & REITs Dominate

• Blackstone, Brookfield, and GIC are investing billions in logistics, life sciences, and commercial properties.

• Real estate investment trusts (REITs) are attracting retail investors globally.

✓ 4. Luxury Housing Surges Amid Economic Uncertainty

· Ultra-rich buyers still invest in premium real estate in London, NYC, Dubai, and Hong Kong.

· Record-breaking sales continue despite global slowdowns.

✓ 5. Sustainable & Smart Real Estate Gains Traction

· Developers are prioritizing green buildings, net-zero carbon skyscrapers, and AI-driven smart homes.

· PropTech innovations (AI, blockchain, smart contracts) are transforming real estate transactions.

Real estate remains one of the most powerful wealth-building industries in the world. The top billionaires of 2023 continue to shape global cities, push architectural boundaries, and redefine investment strategies.

Pro Tip: Understanding how top real estate developers build their wealth can provide valuable insights for investors, homebuyers, and entrepreneurs.

THE ART OF THE DEAL – THE BIGGEST REAL ESTATE TRANSACTIONS IN HISTORY

"Some of the biggest real estate deals in history were made on a handshake. Others ended in bankruptcy." — Real Estate Insider

Real estate is a game of high stakes. Some deals turn ordinary land into billion-dollar assets, while others result in ghost cities, financial disasters, or geopolitical shocks. In this chapter, we dive into the world's most expensive, ambitious, and controversial real estate transactions, examining the lessons they teach investors and developers.

Record-Breaking Residential Sales

1. The Most Expensive Home Ever Sold – Hong Kong's Billionaire Mansion

✓ Property: Mount Nicholson Super-Mansion (Hong Kong)

✓ Price: $2.2 billion (2021)

✓ Buyer: Anonymous Chinese billionaire

✓ Details:

• Located in Hong Kong's Peak District, the world's most expensive residential neighbourhood.

• Sold for $118,000 per sq. ft., double Manhattan's top luxury rates.

Lesson: Ultra-luxury homes remain safe havens for the ultra-rich, even during economic downturns.

2. The U.S. Record-Breaker – 220 Central Park South Penthouse

✓ Price: $238 million (2019)

✓ Buyer: Ken Griffin (CEO of Citadel)

✓ Key Fact:

• Griffin funded the purchase by selling $500 million worth of modern art (Pollock, de Kooning).

• The penthouse set a U.S. home price record, with $23,000/month maintenance fees.

Lesson: New York remains a prime destination for billionaire buyers, regardless of economic cycles.

The Biggest Corporate & Commercial Deals

3. The "Walkie Talkie" Skyscraper Sale – London's $1.8B Office Tower

✓ Property: 20 Fenchurch Street (London, UK)

✓ Price: $1.8 billion (2017)

✓ Buyer: Lee Kum Kee family (Hong Kong's sauce tycoons)

✓ Details:

· 38-story commercial tower in London's financial district.

· The deal was part of a $50B wave of Asian investment in UK real estate pre-Brexit.

Lesson: London remains a global financial hub, attracting Asian wealth despite Brexit uncertainty.

4. India's Largest Office Deal – Embassy Tech Village (Bengaluru)

✓ Price: $2 billion (2020)

✓ Buyer: Blackstone Group

✓ Seller: Embassy Group (Jitendra Virwani)

✓ Details:

· Asia's largest office park deal, covering 10 million sq. ft.

· Houses major companies like Amazon, Microsoft, and Cisco.

Lesson: India's IT and tech outsourcing boom is fueling record commercial property investments.

High-Risk, High-Reward Real Estate Ventures

5. The Plaza Hotel Gamble – Trump's $407M Loss

✓ Property: Plaza Hotel (New York City)

✓ Price: $407.5 million (1988) → $1.4 billion resale (1995)

✓ Buyer: Donald Trump (bought), Saudi Prince Al-Waleed (sold)

✓ Drama:

· Trump borrowed heavily to buy the Plaza, defaulted within 5 years, and lost hundreds of millions.

· The hotel went bankrupt twice but remains an NYC icon (Home Alone 2 filmed here).

Lesson: Overleveraging—even on a trophy asset—can lead to financial disaster.

Grand Vision or Costly Mistake? Megaprojects That Shaped Cities

6. The $500B NEOM Smart City (Saudi Arabia)

✓ Project: NEOM – The Line

✓ Budget: $500 billion (est. 2025 completion)

✓ Visionary: Crown Prince Mohammed bin Salman

✓ Plan:

· A 110-mile-long mirrored skyscraper city, promising flying taxis, AI-run services, and a no-carbon future.

· Critics call it a fantasy, but luxury home pre-sales began in 2023.

Lesson: Ambitious projects attract global attention, but success depends on execution, not hype.

7. Dubai's $14B "World Islands" Disaster

✓ Project: The World Islands (Dubai, UAE)

✓ Cost: $14 billion (2003–2008)

✓ Developer: Nakheel Properties

✓ Status: Mostly abandoned

✓ Backstory:

· A 300-island archipelago shaped like a world map, meant to be billionaire retreats.

· Environmental damage + the 2008 crash left most islands undeveloped.

Lesson: Overambitious luxury projects without real demand often fail spectacularly.

8. China's $5B Ghost City – Thames Town

✓ Property: Thames Town (Shanghai, China)

✓ Cost: $5 billion (2006–2010)

✓ Developer: Shanghai Songjiang New City Construction

✓ Details:

· A full-scale replica of an English village, complete with a Winston Churchill statue.

· Less than 10% occupied due to its remote location.

Lesson: Real estate must align with demand—grand designs alone don't guarantee success.

The Future of Billion-Dollar Real Estate Deals

1. Institutional Investors Will Dominate

✓ Firms like Blackstone, Brookfield, and GIC are buying up data centers, warehouses, and rental housing.

✓ Private equity deals will exceed $100B annually in real estate by 2030.

2. PropTech & AI-Driven Transactions Will Rise

✓ Blockchain & smart contracts will eliminate fraud and speed up billion-dollar deals.

✓ AI will predict high-return locations before mainstream investors.

3. Sustainable & Green Real Estate Will Attract Premium Buyers

✓ Net-zero carbon skyscrapers and eco-friendly cities will become high-value investments.

Key Takeaways from History's Biggest Real Estate Transactions

✓ Big deals don't always mean big profits – Overpaying for status properties can backfire (Plaza Hotel, Thames Town).

✓ Global cities remain prime investment destinations – London, NYC, and Dubai continue to attract billion-dollar deals.

✓ Tech and sustainability are the new frontiers – Data centers, logistics hubs, and green real estate are growing fast.

✓ Political risks impact megaprojects – China's ghost cities and Saudi Arabia's NEOM hinge on government stability.

Final Thoughts

The world's most expensive, ambitious, and sometimes disastrous real estate transactions show that vision, timing, and execution determine success. From billion-dollar mansions to futuristic smart cities, the next decade will see even larger, more technologically advanced real estate deals.

Pro Tip: Whether buying a luxury home, a commercial property, or investing in REITs, understanding real estate history helps avoid costly mistakes.

Donald Trump – The Real Estate Mogul Turned President

"Sometimes by losing a battle, you find a new way to win the war." — *Donald Trump*

Donald John Trump is a figure who redefined real estate, branding, and politics in modern America. From his early days developing luxury skyscrapers to his reality TV fame and two-term presidency, his career is a blend of aggressive deal-making, controversy, and strategic reinvention.

This chapter explores Trump's impact on the real estate industry, his business philosophy, and how he leveraged his empire to shape his political journey.

Early Life and Education

Donald Trump was born on June 14, 1946, in Queens, New York, as the fourth of five children to Fred Trump, a successful real estate developer, and Mary Anne MacLeod Trump.

✓ Education & Early Interest in Business:

• Attended the New York Military Academy for discipline and leadership training.

• Studied at Fordham University before transferring to the Wharton School at the University of Pennsylvania, where he earned a degree in economics (1968).

✓ Influence of Fred Trump:

• Fred Trump built affordable housing in Brooklyn & Queens, amassing a fortune in middle-class real estate.

• Donald inherited his father's real estate expertise but sought to expand into luxury and commercial properties.

Rise in Real Estate – From Queens to Manhattan

Trump officially joined the family business, E. Trump & Son, in 1968, later renaming it The Trump Organization.

✓ Early Projects in Brooklyn & Queens:

• Focused on renovating apartment complexes and securing government-backed loans.

• Learned aggressive negotiation tactics from his father, particularly in securing tax breaks.

✓ Breaking into Manhattan Real Estate:

• In the 1970s, Trump saw Manhattan as the true center of power and shifted focus from outer boroughs.

· Negotiated the Grand Hyatt New York deal (1976), his first major project, securing tax breaks and government financing.

✓ Trump Tower (1983) – His First Signature Skyscraper:

· 68-story luxury tower on Fifth Avenue, home to celebrities, billionaires, and Trump's personal office.

· Branded as ultra-luxurious, redefining the NYC skyline and setting a new standard for real estate marketing.

Business Philosophy & Controversies

✓ "The Art of the Deal" (1987) → Trump's best-selling book outlined his aggressive negotiation tactics, including:

? Maximizing media attention – "Even bad press is good press."

? Using debt as leverage – Borrow big, grow bigger.

? Creating exclusivity through branding – Make properties status symbols, not just buildings.

✓ Real Estate Failures & Bankruptcies:

· Trump's casinos in Atlantic City went bankrupt six times, showing overextension and risky financial maneuvers.

· The Trump Plaza Hotel (bought in 1988 for $407M) was sold at a $300M+ loss.

✓ The Shift to Licensing & Branding:

· By the 1990s, Trump pivoted away from direct ownership toward licensing the "Trump" name to buildings, hotels, and products.

· Trump-branded properties appeared globally (India, Turkey, Philippines) with little financial risk.

Lesson: Trump's success was not just in owning real estate but in selling an image.

Reality TV, Public Persona & Political Ascent

✓ The Apprentice (2004-2015):

· The NBC reality show revitalized Trump's brand, portraying him as a ruthless but decisive businessman.

· "You're Fired" became a cultural catchphrase, boosting his national recognition.

✓ Real Estate Influence on Politics:

· Trump's campaign messaging borrowed from his business playbook:

? "Make America Great Again" = Similar to how he branded his buildings as the best.

? Tax cuts & deregulation → Policies favouring real estate development.

✓ From Businessman to Politician:

· Won the presidency in 2016, leveraging his business empire as proof of his leadership skills.

· Critics argued his real estate empire posed conflicts of interest during his presidency.

· Lost the Election In 2020 to Joe Biden.

· Won the presidency back in 2024 defeating Kamala Harris.

Presidency & Real Estate Impact

✓ Tax Cuts & Deregulation (2017-2021):

· Passed tax reforms benefiting real estate developers, allowing deductions on pass-through income.

· Opportunity Zones program → Encouraged real estate investment in low-income areas.

✓ Conflict of Interest Allegations:

· Critics questioned Trump's hotels & properties profiting from foreign diplomats & government spending.

· The Trump International Hotel (Washington D.C.) became a political hotspot.

✓ Post-Presidency Real Estate Influence:

· Despite political controversies, Trump-branded properties remain luxury symbols.

· The Trump Organization is now led by Donald Jr. & Eric Trump, with Barron Trump rumored to enter real estate.

Global Influence & The Future of Trump's Real Estate Empire

✓ Trump's Real Estate Footprint Across the Globe:

? Trump Towers (India): Luxury apartments in Mumbai, Pune, and Gurgaon.

? Trump Tower (Philippines): Partnered with Filipino billionaires for high-end projects.

? Trump SoHo (New York): Originally marketed as ultra-luxury but later rebranded due to political fallout.

✓ Post-Presidency Business Challenges:

· Several partners rebranded Trump properties due to political backlash.

· New ventures include media and potential real estate expansions in Florida.

✓ Future Speculations:

· Trump-branded residential properties may continue as luxury assets.

· His sons and business empire remain active in real estate, with new licensing deals on the horizon.

Lessons from Trump's Real Estate Journey

✓ Branding is Everything → Trump's name became a real estate status symbol, even when he didn't own the properties.

✓ Debt Can Make or Break You → High leverage led to major expansions but also bankruptcies.

✓ Political Aspirations Can Influence Real Estate → Trump's presidency boosted and hurt his business at the same time.

✓ Adaptability is Key → After financial troubles, Trump reinvented himself in TV, politics, and branding.

Final Thoughts

Donald Trump's legacy in real estate is as controversial as it is influential. From luxury skyscrapers to casinos, global branding, and political dominance, he has used his real estate empire as a launching pad for success in multiple fields.

While some see him as a visionary businessman, others view his strategies as risky and overleveraged. Either way, his imprint on the real estate industry remains undeniable, with his brand continuing to influence luxury real estate, global marketing, and investment trends.

Pro Tip: For investors, Trump's journey shows the power of branding, calculated risk-taking, and media influence in real estate.